American
ENGLISH FILE

Workbook

Christina Latham-Koenig
Clive Oxenden
Paul Seligson

Paul Seligson and Clive Oxenden are the original co-authors of
English File 1 and *English File 2*

OXFORD
UNIVERSITY PRESS

Contents

STUDY LINK iChecker SELF-ASSESSMENT CD-ROM

Powerful listening and interactive assessment CD-ROM

Your iChecker disc on the inside back cover of this Workbook includes:

- **AUDIO** – Download ALL of the audio files for the Listening and Pronunciation activities in this Workbook for on-the-go listening practice.
- **FILE TESTS** – Check your progress by taking a self-assessment test after you complete each File.

Audio: When you see this symbol **iChecker**, go to the iChecker disc in the back of this Workbook. Load the disc in your computer.

1

Type your name and press "ENTER."

2

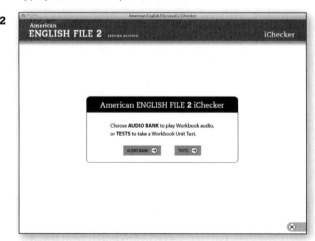

Choose "AUDIO BANK."

3

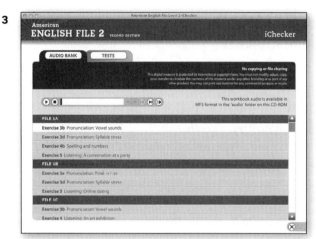

Click on the exercise for the File. Then use the media player to listen.

You can transfer the audio to a mobile device from the "audio" folder on the disc.

File test: At the end of every File, there is a test. To do the test, load the iChecker and select "Tests." Select the test for the File you have just finished.

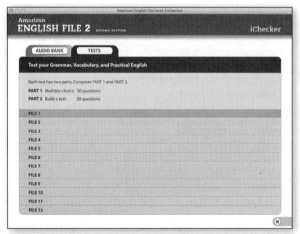

1A Where are you from?

1 GRAMMAR word order in questions

a Put the words in the parentheses into the correct place in the questions.

1 Where you born? (were)
   *Where **were** you born?*

2 Do have any brothers or sisters? (you)
   _____

3 What college you go to? (do)
   _____

4 What languages you speak? (can)
   _____

5 Where you study English before? (did)
   _____

6 What kind of music do you listen? (to)
   _____

7 How do you exercise? (often)
   _____

8 Where did you last weekend? (go)
   _____

b Write questions in the simple present or past.

1 Where *do you go to college* ?
   (you / go to college)
2 What _____?
   (you / do last night)
3 What _____?
   (TV shows / your family / watch)
4 When _____?
   (your birthday)
5 Where _____?
   (you / from)
6 Where _____?
   (your friends / go / vacation last year)
7 What kind of books _____?
   (you / read)
8 Why _____?
   (you / angry yesterday)

2 VOCABULARY common verb phrases

Match the verbs and nouns.

1 be born — [j]   a MTV, a TV show
2 do — []   b in a house, with friends
3 listen to — []   c two sisters, a pet
4 play — []   d yoga, karate
5 read — []   e an email, a magazine
6 speak — []   f to the movies, on vacation
7 live — []   g the guitar, basketball
8 watch — []   h a foreign language, English
9 go — []   i dance music, R&B
10 have — []   j in Toronto, in Canada

3 PRONUNCIATION vowel sounds, the alphabet

a Circle the letter with a different vowel sound.

1 train /eɪ/	2 train /eɪ/	3 tree /i/	4 tree /i/	5 egg /ɛ/	6 egg /ɛ/	7 boot /u/
A	H	G	M	N	X	Q
K	P	V	C	B	S	I
Ⓔ	J	R	D	F	K	U

b iChecker Listen and check. Then listen again and repeat the letters.

c Underline the stressed syllables in these words.

1 in|stru|ment
2 bas|ket|ball
3 thir|teen
4 thir|ty
5 co|llege
6 week|end
7 ma|ga|zine
8 sis|ter
9 lan|guage
10 a|ddress

d iChecker Listen and check. Then listen again and repeat the words.

4 SPELLING AND NUMBERS

a Continue the series.

1 nine, ten, _____*eleven*_____, _____*twelve*_____
2 fifteen, sixteen, _____, _____
3 sixty, seventy, _____, _____
4 ninety-eight, ninety-nine, _____, _____
5 six hundred, seven hundred, _____, _____
6 three hundred and fifty, four hundred, _____, _____
7 one thousand, three thousand, _____, _____
8 ten thousand, twenty thousand, _____, _____

b iChecker Listen and write the words.

1 ____*parents*____   6 _____
2 _____   7 _____
3 _____   8 _____
4 _____   9 _____
5 _____   10 _____

5 LISTENING

a iChecker Listen to a conversation between two people at a party. Why does Ben leave?

_____

b iChecker Listen again. Mark the sentences T (true) or F (false).

1 Sandra is a nurse.   _T_
2 Ben is a doctor.   ___
3 Sandra likes dance music.   ___
4 Sandra didn't go to the Muse concert. ___
5 Sandra plays tennis.   ___
6 Ben plays soccer.   ___

USEFUL WORDS AND PHRASES

Learn these words and phrases.

get in touch with /gɛt ɪn tʌtʃ wɪð/
go to bed early /goʊ tə bɛd ˈərli/
have (sth) in common /hæv ɪn ˈkɑmən/
last weekend /læst ˈwikɛnd/
spend time on (sth) /spɛnd taɪm ɑn/
somewhere nice /ˈsʌmwɛr naɪs/
How often do you…? /haʊ ˈɑfn də yu/
What kind of (music)…? /wɑt ˈkaɪnd əv/
Where were you born? /ˈwɛr ˈwər yu ˈbɔrn/

1 GRAMMAR simple present

a Write negative sentences.

1 You get up early.   *You don't get up early* .
2 It rains a lot here.   _____ .
3 We live in a house.   _____ .
4 I play tennis.   _____ .
5 He has a beard.   _____ .
6 They go to the gym.   _____ .
7 She writes a blog.   _____ .

b Complete the questions with *do* or *does*.

1 When __*do*__ you meet your friends?
2 _____ your laptop have a webcam?
3 What time _____ we need to leave?
4 _____ your mother work from home?
5 Which websites _____ you use most?
6 _____ your best friend like action movies?
7 _____ your brother spend a lot of time on Facebook?

c Complete the text with the correct form of the verbs in the box.

not come	earn	get along	study	invite	not like
live	prefer	not see	share	want	~~work~~

I am very different from my best friend, Tabitha. Tabitha [1] __*works*__ as a nurse, and she [2] _____ a lot of money. I'm a student, and I [3] _____ music in college. I [4] _____ to be a music teacher.

Tabitha [5] _____ in a small house in the country, and I [6] _____ an apartment with some friends in the city. We often [7] _____ friends for dinner, but Tabitha [8] _____. She's really shy, so she [9] _____ being with other people. I'm very extroverted, so I [10] _____ to be in a group.

I [11] _____ Tabitha much because she's usually busy. But when we're together, we always [12] _____ really well. Some people say that opposites attract, and for me and my best friend Tabitha, it's true.

2 VOCABULARY describing people

Appearance

a Complete the sentences.

1 Does your sister have br__*own*__ eyes or bl__*ue*__ eyes?
2 Tanya's dad doesn't have any hair. He's b_____.
3 My best friend's hair isn't str_____. It's c_____.
4 Andy doesn't shave. He has a b_____ and a m_____.
5 You aren't f_____ at all. I think you're very sl_____.
6 When Jake was young, he was very th_____, but now he's a little ov_____.
7 My hair isn't brown, it's r_____. And I'm not short, I'm m_____ h_____.

Personality

b Complete the opposites.

1 talkative   _____*quiet*_____
2 shy   _____
3 generous   _____
4 friendly   _____
5 hardworking   _____
6 kind   _____
7 serious   _____
8 stupid   _____

c Match the questions 1–6 with the answers a–f.

1 What did you look like when you were a child? [c]
2 What does your husband look like? [ ]
3 What's your best friend like? [ ]
4 What does your sister look like? [ ]
5 What's George like? [ ]
6 What were you like when you were at school? [ ]

a She's tall and slim with long blond hair.
b He's very kind and hardworking.
c ~~I had short curly hair, and I was overweight.~~
d He has short dark hair and a mustache.
e She's smart and really extroverted.
f I was very talkative and a little lazy.

3 PRONUNCIATION final -s / -es

a **iChecker** Listen and circle the verb with a different sound.

1 snake	2 snake	3 zebra	4 zebra	5 /ɪz/	6 /ɪz/
works laughs (watches)	lives thinks drinks	knows rains likes	runs starts goes	leaves dresses washes	teaches cooks misses

b **iChecker** Listen again and repeat the words.

c Underline the stressed syllable.

1 tal|ka|tive
2 ex|tro|ver|ted
3 un|friend|ly
4 ge|ne|rous
5 mu|stache
6 ser|i|ous
7 cur|ly
8 qui|et
9 o|ver|weight

d **iChecker** Listen and check. Then listen again and repeat the words.

4 READING

a Read the article. What happens on "Singles' Day" in Shanghai?

"Singles' Day" in Shanghai

November 11 is "Singles' Day" in Shanghai, and every year a dating event takes place where all the single men and women of the city have the chance to meet a partner. Last year, it was so popular that the organizers had to close online registration because there were no more places.

Between 10,000 and 40,000 people attend the event every year. It's held in a district of Shanghai called Thames Town. At least 50 dating agencies take part. They set up stands in the town hall with billboards displaying cards with the height, birth date, education, and annual income of thousands of clients. People who did not manage to register for the event organize their own unofficial dating system by writing their names and phone numbers on pieces of paper and attaching them to the fence outside the town hall.

More people take part in "Singles' Day" every year because of the growing number of single adults in Shanghai. In the city, more than 24 percent of people over the age of 15 are unmarried.

b Read the article again. Mark the sentences T (true) or F (false).

1 The people who take part in "Singles' Day" aren't married.   *T*

2 Many people register for the event on the Internet.   __

3 All of the dating events are in the town hall.   __

4 People who don't register for the event can't find a partner on "Singles' Day."   __

5 Every year, there are more single adults in Shanghai.   __

c Underline five words you don't know. Check their meaning and pronunciation with a dictionary.

5 LISTENING

a **iChecker** Listen to a radio program about online dating. How many people call the program? _____

b **iChecker** Listen again and match the callers with the sentences A–F.

1 Alan   *C*   __

2 Kate   __   __

3 Paolo   __   __

A He / She doesn't have time for a social life.

B He / She made a mistake.

C ~~He / She got engaged with the partner he / she met online.~~

D He / She married someone who was married before.

E He / She doesn't like meeting new people.

F He / She is happily married now, but doesn't have any children.

USEFUL WORDS AND PHRASES

Learn these words and phrases.

guy /gaɪ/

partner /ˈpɑrtnər/

single person /ˈsɪŋɡl ˈpərsn/

smile /smaɪl/

sociable /ˈsoʊʃəbl/

be into (sth) /bi ˈɪntə/

feel like (doing something) /fil laɪk/

get along well (with) /ɡɛt əˈlɔŋ wɛl/

go on a date /ɡoʊ ɑn ə deɪt/

sense of humor /sɛns əv ˈhyumər/

1C Mr. and Mrs. Clark and Percy

1 VOCABULARY

clothes

a Complete the crossword.

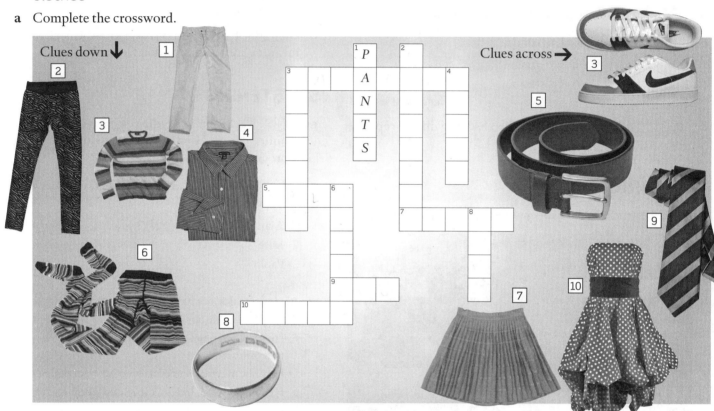

Clues down ↓

Clues across →

prepositions of place

b Look at the painting. Complete the sentences with these prepositions.

| on the left | ~~in~~ | between |
| in front of | next to | behind |

1 There are many people __*in*__ the picture.

2 There are some boats _____ of the picture.

3 There are two small animals _____ the woman and man with an umbrella.

4 A small girl in a white dress is _____ the woman in the middle of the painting.

5 A black dog is _____ the man with a beard.

6 There is a woman _____ the two men sitting down.

2 GRAMMAR present continuous

a Look at the painting again. Read the museum guide's description of it. Write the verbs in the present continuous.

***Sunday Afternoon on the Island of La Grande Jatte,
1884–86, Georges-Pierre Seurat***

As you can see, the sun ¹ *is shining* in this picture, and the people ² _____ (relax) by the Seine River in Paris. On the right of the picture, a man and a woman ³ _____ (walk) their pets. On the left, a man ⁴ _____ (lie) on the grass. He looks like he ⁵ _____ (relax). In the middle of the picture, two girls ⁶ _____ (sit) down. What ⁷ _____ (they / do)? Maybe they ⁸ _____ (wait) for some friends? Or maybe they ⁹ _____ (watch) the other people? On the right, near the trees, there is another girl. She ¹⁰ _____ (play) with someone, but we can't see who it is.

b Complete the sentences with the simple present or present continuous form of the verbs in the box.

drink	drive	like	~~listen~~	live	rain	sleep	study	wear	work

1 Sorry, I can't hear you. I *'m listening* to music.
2 Charles always _____ to work.
3 "Shhhh! Be quiet! The children _____."
4 We can't play tennis today. It _____.
5 Fiona _____ four cups of coffee every day.
6 We _____ this picture very much.
7 My brother _____ in the music industry.
8 Kathy always _____ jeans at home.
9 They can't come to the movies because they _____ for the exam tomorrow.
10 My parents _____ in a big house.

3 PRONUNCIATION /ə/ and /ər/

a Write the words in the chart.

| attractive | third | cardigan | skirt | sweater | bracelet |
| prefer | jacket | necklace | problem | T-shirt | world |

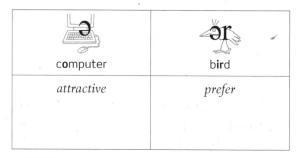

computer	bird
attractive	*prefer*

b iChecker Listen and check. Then listen again and repeat the words.

4 LISTENING

a iChecker Listen to an advertisement for an art exhibition. What is special about the pictures?

_____

b iChecker Listen again and answer the questions.

1 Where is the David Hockney exhibition?

_____

2 What was the first picture he drew on his iPhone?

_____

3 What does he do with his flower pictures?

_____

4 When is the last day of the exhibition?

_____

5 How much does the exhibition cost?

_____

USEFUL WORDS AND PHRASES

Learn these words and phrases.

feet /fit/
knee /ni/
portrait /ˈpɔrtrət/
poster /ˈpoʊstər/
pregnant /ˈprɛgnənt/
relationship /rɪˈleɪʃnʃɪp/
unusual /ʌnˈyuʒuəl/
close together /kloʊs təˈgɛðər/

iChecker **TESTS** FILE 1

1 CALLING RECEPTION

Complete the conversation with a phrase from the box.

> I have a problem with the Wi-Fi.
> I'll put you through to IT.
> I'll send somebody up right away.
> I'm sorry to bother you again.
> There's a problem with the shower.
> ~~This is room 402.~~

A Hello, reception.
B Hello. ⁰ *This is room 402.*
A How can I help you?
B ² _____ There isn't any hot water.
A I'm sorry, ma'am. ³ _____
B Thank you.

A Good morning, reception.
B Hello. ⁴ _____ This is room 402.
A How can I help you?
B ⁵ _____ I can't get a signal.
A I'm sorry, ma'am. ⁶ _____
B Thanks.

2 SOCIAL ENGLISH

Complete the missing words in the conversation.

1 **A** So, here you are a*t* l*ast*.
  B Yes. It's great to be here.

2 **A** Do you have a g_____ v_____?
  B Yes. I can see the Empire State Building from my window.

3 **A** William is l_____ f_____ to meeting you.
  B Really? Who's William?

4 **A** It's time to go. You m_____ b_____ really tired.
  B I guess you're right.

5 **A** B_____ t_____ w_____, it's great to see you again.
  B Yes. It's great to see you, too.

3 READING

a Read the advertisement and mark the sentences T (true) or F (false).

1 The Park Central New York is in the center of the city.   _T_
2 It's near major tourist attractions.   ___
3 It's very comfortable.   ___
4 All rooms have free Wi-Fi access.   ___
5 The hotel's restaurant is not very expensive.   ___
6 The hotel has a free parking lot.   ___
7 The staff only speaks English.   ___

Park Central New York Hotel
New York

Our facilities and services:
- in-room safe
- in-room Wi-Fi (surcharge)
- electronic checkout
- parking garage (surcharge)
- room service
- on-site car rental
- gift shop

"Great location and service"

Located in the heart of the city, the Park Central New York is in easy walking distance of Carnegie Hall, Broadway, and the Museum of Modern Art (MOMA). Central Park is only three blocks away. Fifth Avenue, with its international boutiques and huge department stores, is only a ten-minute walk from the hotel. For guests who want to travel farther away, there are seven subway lines located within three blocks of the hotel.

The Park Central New York offers great service, great comfort, and great value. The hotel's bistro, Cityhouse, provides the perfect setting for dinner before a concert or a Broadway show in the evening. Guests can enjoy the reasonably priced specials menu while watching the world go by on Seventh Avenue through the bistro's oversized windows.

Because of its central location, the Park Central New York is the ideal hotel for tourists visiting the city for the first time. Our multi-lingual staff at the front desk is always happy to provide tour assistance and answer any questions guests may have.

b Underline five words you don't know. Use your dictionary to look up their pronunciation and meaning.

> A vacation is having nothing to do and all day to do it in.
>
> *Robert Orben, American magician and comedy writer*

2A Right place, wrong person

1 VOCABULARY vacations

a Write the phrases.

1 go *camping*
2 go _____ a _____
3 _____ flights on the Internet
4 go _____
5 _____ skis
6 go _____ at night
7 _____ in a hotel
8 go _____
9 _____ on the beach
10 go _____ for the weekend

b Complete the sentences with an adjective.

1 We loved our room. It was very c_*omfortable*__.
2 The weather was warm and s_____ every day.
3 There were a lot of people everywhere. It was very cr_____.
4 We ate very well. The food was d_____.
5 The staff at the hotel was horrible. They were very unh_____, and sometimes very rude.
6 There wasn't much in the apartment. It was very b_____. It didn't even have a refrigerator.
7 The other people on the trip were very fr_____.We hope to meet some of them again in the future.
8 The town was n_____. All the houses had flowers on the balcony and were painted different colors.
9 It was cl_____, and we didn't see the sun at all.
10 Our first meal was d_____, so we didn't eat at the hotel again.

2 GRAMMAR simple past: regular and irregular verbs

a Write the simple past of these verbs in the correct column.

~~argue~~	~~begin~~	arrive	ask	buy	can	choose
eat	feel	invite	rent	say	stay	sunbathe

Regular	Irregular
argued	*began*
_____	_____
_____	_____
_____	_____
_____	_____
_____	_____

b Make the verbs negative.

1 We stayed at a campsite.
   _____*We didn't stay*_____ in a hotel.
2 They bought postcards.
   _____ any souvenirs.
3 The people were unfriendly.
   _____ very helpful.
4 I sunbathed on the beach.
   _____ by the pool.
5 We rented bikes.
   _____ a car.
6 He spent a month in Bangkok.
   _____ a week there.
7 Our room was dirty.
   _____ very clean.

11

c Complete the text with the simple past form of the verbs in the box.

arrive ask book cannot ~~decide~~ go (x2) look take want

The vacation that wasn't

Four years ago, we ¹ _decided_ to go away for the weekend. We
² _____ to go to Mexico, so we ³ _____ a beautiful
apartment online. A week later, we ⁴ _____ a taxi to the
airport. We ⁵ _____ at the airport at two o'clock, and we
⁶ _____ to check in. The woman at the desk ⁷ _____
us for our passports. We ⁸ _____ in our bags, but we
⁹ _____ find them. So we ¹⁰ _____ home!

d Read the text in **c** again. Complete the questions.

1 When _did they decide_ to go away for the weekend? Four years ago.
2 Where _____ to go? Mexico.
3 How _____ the apartment? They booked it online.
4 When _____ at the airport? At two o'clock.
5 What _____ ask for? She asked for their passports.
6 Where _____ in the end? They went back home.

3 PRONUNCIATION -ed endings, irregular verbs

a iChecker Listen and circle the verb that has a different -ed sound.

1 walked   asked   (rented)
2 argued   wanted   stayed
3 booked   started   decided
4 arrived   invited   sunbathed

b iChecker Listen again and repeat the words.

c Write these irregular simple past forms in the correct circle.

~~bought~~ ~~broke~~ ~~called~~ ~~came~~ ~~caught~~ drank ~~drove~~ ~~made~~
~~rang~~ read ~~said~~ sat ~~went~~ wrote ~~gave~~

1 **saw** — ɔ
bought
_____
_____

2 **cat** — æ
drank
_____
_____

3 **phone** — oʊ
broke
_____
_____

4 **egg** — ɛ
read
_____
_____

5 **train** — eɪ
came
_____
_____

d iChecker Listen and check. Then listen again and repeat the words.

4 LISTENING

iChecker Listen to five speakers talking about vacations they didn't enjoy. Which speaker...?

a didn't have a very exciting weekend ___
b wasn't with the people he / she wanted to be with _1_
c chose a vacation destination because of the weather there ___
d went on vacation after a relationship ended ___
e didn't feel well when he / she was on vacation ___

~~Speaker 1~~   Speaker 2   Speaker 3

Speaker 4   Speaker 5

USEFUL WORDS AND PHRASES

Learn these words and phrases.

atmosphere /ˈætməsfɪr/
disaster /dɪˈzæstər/
hostels /ˈhɑstlz/
complain /kəmˈpleɪn/
enjoy /ɪnˈdʒɔɪ/
flirt /flərt/
view /vyu/
break up /ˈbreɪk ʌp/
feel sorry for (somebody) /fil ˈsɑri fər/
go wrong /goʊ rɔŋ/

Photographs are pictures taken to please
the family and bore the neighbors.
Edmund Volkart, American sociologist

2B The story behind the photo

1 GRAMMAR past continuous

a Complete the sentences with the verbs in parentheses in the past continuous.

1 You __were laughing__ (laugh) when I took the photo.
2 It _____ (snow) when our plane landed.
3 We _____ (not drive) fast when the accident happened.
4 What _____ (he / do) when his boss arrived?
5 Why _____ (you / cry) at the party?
6 I _____ (sit) on the bus when I saw my boss.
7 They _____ (live) in Brazil when their first child was born.
8 He didn't call you because his cell phone _____ (not work).

b Write sentences with *when*. Use the simple past
and past continuous.

1 They / argue / the waiter /
bring / the check
They were arguing when
the waiter brought the check.

2 He / fall / off his bike /
cycle / home
_____
_____ .

3 The children / play / video
games / the guests / arrive
_____
_____ .

4 We / have / a barbecue /
it / start / to rain
_____
_____ .

5 I / finish / my report / my
computer / crash
_____
_____ .

c Complete the story with the simple past or
past continuous.

Last summer, I [1] __went__ (go) to Los Angeles to stay
with my cousin for a few weeks. One afternoon, we
[2] _____ (have) lunch in a nice restaurant
when my cousin [3] _____ (get) a call on her cell
phone and went outside to talk. While she
[4] _____ (speak) to her friend, I suddenly
[5] _____ (notice) a man in a black hat who
[6] _____ (sit) at the next table. It was the actor
Johnny Depp! He was alone, and I [7] _____ (decide)
to take my chance. So I got up and [8] _____ (go)
to his table. "Excuse me, could I have my photo taken
with you?" I asked. He [9] _____ (say) yes, so I
[10] _____ (stop) a waitress who [11] _____ (pass)
by and gave her my camera. She [12] _____ (take)
the photo of me and Johnny. I thanked them both, and then I
returned to my table. When my cousin [13] _____ (come)
back, I [14] _____ (smile).

"Why are you looking so happy?" she asked.

"I had my photo taken with Johnny Depp."

"Johnny Depp? Where is he?"

"He's sitting over there. Look!'

She turned around to look and then started to laugh.

"That's not Johnny Depp!"

I [15] _____ (look) at the man in the black hat – he
[16] _____ (laugh), too.

2 VOCABULARY at, in, on

time

a Complete the sentences with *at*, *in*, or *on*.

1 The results of the election were announced __at__ 11 o'clock.

2 Cell phones were invented _____ the 20th century.

3 Our flight is leaving _____ Wednesday at 9:30 _____ the evening and arriving _____ 12 o'clock _____ Thursday.

4 We have an exam _____ Monday morning.

5 In most countries, banks and offices are closed _____ New Year's Day.

6 I hate driving _____ night, getting up early _____ the morning, and working _____ the weekend.

7 Steve Jobs was born _____ 1955, and he died _____ October 5, 2011.

8 We went to Florida last winter, and we're going again _____ the summer, probably the last two weeks _____ July.

place

b Complete the sentences with *at*, *in*, or *on*.

1 He took some great photos __at__ the party.

2 I can't read a book _____ the bus or _____ a car.

3 We want to put some shelves _____ the wall _____ the living room. We're going to put all our old books _____ the shelves.

4 My family is from Brazil, but we live _____ New York, _____ the 11th floor of a tall building.

5 I'll meet you _____ the bus stop.

6 The adults sat _____ chairs and the children sat _____ the floor.

7 They spent the morning _____ the museum and then went for a walk _____ the park.

8 Please meet me _____ the library by the front desk _____ noon.

3 PRONUNCIATION sentence stress

iChecker Listen and repeat the dialogue. Copy the rhythm.

A **Where** were **you** at **ten** o'**clock** last **night**?
B I was at **home**.
A **What** were you **doing**?
B I was **watching** a **movie**.

4 LISTENING

a iChecker Listen to a conversation between Matt and Jenny about a photo. Does Jenny like the photo? _____

b iChecker Listen again and choose the best answers.

1 The photo shows…
  a Matt's parents.
  b Matt's aunt and uncle.
  c Matt's grandparents.

2 The photo was taken…
  a in the spring.
  b in the summer.
  c in the fall.

3 The man wanted to win…
  a some money.
  b some food.
  c some jewelry.

4 The other people in the photo were the man's…
  a neighbors.
  b friends.
  c colleagues.

5 The man in the stall…
  a took the photo.
  b asked for more money for the photo.
  c didn't like the photo.

USEFUL WORDS AND PHRASES

Learn these words and phrases.

democracy /dɪˈmɑkrəsi/
demonstration /dɛmənˈstreɪʃn/
election /ɪˈlɛkʃn/
freedom /ˈfridəm/
hold hands /hoʊld hændz/
peace /pis/
realize /ˈriəlaɪz/
TV screens /ˈti ˈvi skrinz/
upload /ˈʌploʊd/
screen saver /skrin ˈseɪvər/

2C One dark October evening

1 GRAMMAR time sequencers and connectors

a (Circle) the correct words or phrases.

¹**The summer** /(**One summer**), I decided to travel to Peru. I flew to Lima, and then traveled to a town near Machu Picchu to spend the night. ²**The next day** / **Afterday**, I climbed the mountain to visit the monument. I was tired ³**when** / **then** I reached the top. ⁴**Sudden** / **Suddenly**, I saw a man who was in my English class back home. ⁵**Two minutes later** / **Two minutes after**, he came over to speak to me, and he was just as surprised as I was. ⁶**After that** / **When**, we decided to travel together. We had a great summer, and we continued seeing each other back home. In fact, we got married two years later, and we now have a beautiful daughter named Hannah.

b Look at each group of sentences. Complete each sentence with *so*, *because*, *but*, or *although*.

1 a Linda ran to the train station __because__ she was very late.
  b Linda was very late, _____ she ran to the train station.
  c _____ Linda ran to the train station, she was too late and she missed the train.
2 a _____ we couldn't go out, we had a really good afternoon at home.
  b It was raining _____ we stayed at home.
  c We stayed at home last Sunday _____ it was raining.
3 a The tickets were really expensive, _____ they managed to sell them all in an hour.
  b _____ the tickets were really expensive, they sold them all in an hour.
  c They sold the tickets quickly _____ the concert was very popular.

c Rewrite the sentences using the words in parentheses.

1 I didn't have any breakfast because I didn't have time. **(so)**
  I didn't have time, __*so I didn't have any breakfast*__.
2 I had a great vacation in Egypt although I can't speak Arabic. **(but)**
  I can't speak Arabic, _____
  _____.
3 I don't really like Ryan, but I went to lunch with him. **(although)**
  I went to lunch with Ryan _____
  _____.
4 I called the police because the door to my apartment was open. **(so)**
  The door to my apartment was open, _____
  _____.
5 Jim has a lot of money, but he's really cheap. **(although)**
  Jim's really cheap, _____
  _____.
6 Mary couldn't find her bag, so she canceled her credit cards. **(because)**
  Mary canceled her credit cards _____
  _____.

2 VOCABULARY verb phrases

a Match the phrases.

1	Jake and Beth met	*d*	a	her to dinner.
2	He played		b	for her at the door.
3	She left		c	a wonderful evening.
4	He waited		d	~~in a cafe~~.
5	She gave		e	to a new restaurant.
6	He invited		f	the cafe very late.
7	He took her		g	her favorite song.
8	They had		h	him her phone number.

b Cover the right-hand column. Try to remember the sentences.

3 PRONUNCIATION word stress

a Write the words in the chart.

a|cross	af|ter	a|gain	al|though	aw|ful	be|cause
birth|day	eve|ning	in|vite	per|fect	res|tau|rant	se|cond

1 First syllable stressed	2 Second syllable stressed
after	*across*

b **iChecker** Listen and check. Then listen again and repeat the words.

4 READING

a Read the story. Number the paragraphs in the right order.

A lucky escape

☐ Ten minutes later, it began to rain. Soon, Liz found it hard to see out of the front windshield . There was a lot of water on the road, so she drove more slowly. Although Liz was an experienced driver, she felt afraid.

☐ An hour later, firefighters cut Liz out of the car. She went to the hospital, but the doctors sent her home because she didn't have any serious injuries. Her head was fine and she only had a few cuts and bruises . Her son went to collect the groceries from the car and gave the loaf of bread to his mother. Now, she is going to keep it as a souvenir.

1 One day last November, Liz Douglas decided to go grocery shopping. She drove to the supermarket and spent the morning doing her weekly shopping . She paid for her groceries , went back to the parking lot, and put the shopping bags on the back seat of the car. Then she started to drive home.

☐ However, Liz was lucky. When she braked, a loaf of bread flew out of one of the shopping bags. The car turned over, and the loaf of bread landed between Liz's head and the roof of the car. It stopped her head from hitting the car roof.

☐ Suddenly, she lost control of the car. She saw a telephone pole in front of her and braked. She closed her eyes and hoped that the airbags in the car would inflate. Unfortunately, they didn't.

b Look at the highlighted words. What do you think they mean? Check with your dictionary.

5 LISTENING

iChecker Listen to a radio program about people who had lucky escapes. Mark the sentences T (true) or F (false).

1 Maureen Evason was on vacation when the accident happened. _T_

2 She was in the hospital for four months. ___

3 Joseph Rabadue was sitting on the floor when the accident happened. ___

4 The truck hit the TV. ___

5 Barry McRoy was drinking coffee when the fight happened. ___

6 The DVD was in his jacket pocket. ___

USEFUL WORDS AND PHRASES

Learn these words and phrases.

anniversary /ænə'vərsəri/

brake /breɪk/

perfect /'pərfɪkt/

as usual /əz 'yuʒuəl/

cross the street /krɔs ðə strit/

Bridge Street /'brɪdʒ strit/

happy ending /'hæpi 'ɛndɪŋ/

just in time /dʒʌst ɪn 'taɪm/

madly in love /'mædli ɪn lʌv/

until the last minute /ən'tɪl ðə læst 'mɪnət/

iChecker **TESTS** FILE 2

16

I'd like to fly. Then I wouldn't have to wait in airport security lines.

Jim Morris, American baseball player

3A Plans and dreams

1 GRAMMAR *be going to* (plans and predictions)

a Complete the sentences with *going to* + a verb from the box.

be   book   not fly   get   ~~miss~~   need   not sleep   not stay

1 He *'s going to miss* the flight.

2 I _____ my flight online.

3 He _____ during the flight.

4 How _____ she _____ to the airport?

5 That plane _____ today.

6 They _____ late.

7 I _____ in a hotel.

8 _____ we _____ a cart?

b Complete the dialogue with *going to* + the verbs.

Jenny 1 *Are you going to take* (you/take) a vacation this summer?

Philip Yes, but 2 _____ (we / not / go) to the Caribbean. 3 _____ (we / go) to Canada!

Jenny When 4 _____ (you / travel)?

Philip In August. 5 _____ (we / be) there for two weeks.

Jenny What 6 _____ (you / do) while you're there?

Philip 7 _____ (we / stay) in Vancouver for a week, and then 8 _____ (we / rent) a car and visit the Canadian Rockies.

Jenny 9 _____ (it / be) sunny in Toronto in August?

Philip I don't know. But I hope 10 _____ (it / not / rain) too much!

2 VOCABULARY airports

Complete the text.

Last summer, I flew to New York City with my husband to visit some friends. The flight left from 1Terminal 1, so my brother dropped us outside the building. We went inside and looked for the 2e_____ to take us upstairs to 3D_____. We picked up our boarding passes at 4Ch_____. Then we did some shopping. After that, we made our way to the 5g_____ to board our plane. We had a good flight, but we were very tired when we landed at JFK Airport. There was a long line at 6P_____ C_____, and they asked us a lot of questions at Immigration. Finally, we went to 7B_____ C_____ to pick up our bags. We needed a 8c_____ this time because of all our suitcases. Nobody stopped us at 9C_____, so we went straight to 10A_____, where our friends were waiting for us.

3 PRONUNCIATION sentence stress and fast speech

iChecker Listen and repeat. <u>C</u>opy the <u>rh</u>ythm.

1 **Are** they **going** to **meet** you at the **airport**?
2 I **think** we're **going** to be **late**.
3 I'm **not going** to **forget** my **passport**.
4 **What time** are you **going** to **arrive**?
5 She's **going** to **take** the **elevator**.

4 READING

a Read the text. How many airports is Beijing going to have in 2020? _____

b Read the text again. Mark the sentences T (true) or F (false).

1 More than 54 million people use Atlanta International Airport each year.   *F*
2 Atlanta International isn't going to be the busiest airport in 2020.   —
3 A new airport was built for the 2008 Olympic Games.   —
4 Beijing Capital Airport is too small.   —
5 In the future, Beijing's subway is going to reach the new airport.   —
6 The new airport is going to have eight runways.   —

c Look at the highlighted words. What do you think they mean? Check with your dictionary.

5 LISTENING

a **iChecker** Listen to five conversations at the airport. Match the speakers with the places in the box.

~~Arrivals~~	Baggage claim	Check-in
Customs	Immigration	

Dialogue 1   *Arrivals*
Dialogue 2   _____
Dialogue 3   _____
Dialogue 4   _____
Dialogue 5   _____

b **iChecker** Listen again and answer the questions.

1 What did the man eat on the plane?
2 What's the gate number?
3 What's the friend's phone number?
4 What color is the suitcase?
5 What did the woman buy?

The World's Biggest Airport

The world's busiest airport today is in the US. Nearly 54 million passengers pass through Hartsfield-Jackson Atlanta International Airport every year. However, by the end of the next decade, there's going to be a new airport even bigger and busier than Atlanta. The new airport is going to be in the capital of China: Beijing.

Beijing already has two airports. The first is Beijing Capital International Airport, where an extra terminal was built for the 2008 Olympic Games. The second is Beijing Nanyuan Airport, which is mainly used by military planes. Just over 73 million passengers passed through Beijing Capital Airport last year, making it the second busiest after Atlanta. But the current airport is not big enough for all the Chinese passengers who want to travel by plane. This is why the government is going to build a new one.

The new airport is going to be in the suburb of Daxing, in the south of the city. Daxing is about an hour's drive from the center of the city. The government is going to extend Beijing's subway so that passengers can reach it more easily. There are also plans for a high-speed train line. The airport is going to have eight runways for commercial flights, and a ninth runway for military use. This is going to make it the biggest and the busiest airport in the world.

USEFUL WORDS AND PHRASES

Learn these words and phrases.

dreams /drimz/
facilities /fəˈsɪlətiz/
paradise /ˈpærədaɪs/
passenger /ˈpæsəndʒər/
security /sɪˈkyʊrəti/
traveler /ˈtrævələr/

board /bɔrd/
delayed /dɪˈleɪd/
free (Wi-Fi) /fri/
connecting flight /kəˈnɛktɪŋ flaɪt/

The future belongs to those who believe
in the beauty of their dreams.
Eleanor Roosevelt

3B Let's meet again

1 GRAMMAR present continuous (future arrangements)

a Complete the text with the present continuous form of the verbs in parentheses.

"Hi, I'm Lisa, your guide, and I'm going to tell you about the arrangements for your trip to New York City. We ¹ *'re starting* (start) our trip in about five minutes, so please make yourselves comfortable. We ² _____ (drive) you straight to the city – we ³ _____ (not stop) for breakfast on the way. We ⁴ _____ (see) the popular Broadway show *Wicked* today. When we arrive, we ⁵ _____ (drop) you off at Eighth Avenue and 46th Street. We ⁶ _____ (not take) you to Fifth Avenue because the traffic is terrible. We ⁷ _____ (arrive) at 11:30, so you have time for lunch or some shopping before the show begins. The bus driver ⁸ _____ (stay) with the bus all day, so it's OK to leave your coats on the bus. We ⁹ _____ (pick) you up near the theater after the show ends. We ¹⁰ _____ (leave) at 4:45 promptly, so don't be late. Now, any questions?"

b Circle the correct verb form. If both forms are possible, check (✓) the sentence.

1 **A** Why are you looking so worried?
   B I'm sure **I'm going to get** / **I'm getting** lost.

2 **A** Do you have any plans for this weekend?
   B Yes, **I'm going to visit** / **I'm visiting** my grandparents on Sunday.

3 **A** I'm going to Boston next week.
   B Really? Do you think **it's going to be** / **it's being** cold?

4 **A** My brother has a job interview in Tokyo.
   B Oh. Do you think **he's going to get** / **he's getting** the job?

5 **A** What time's the train?
   B At 7:15. Don't worry. We **aren't going to miss** / **aren't missing** it.

6 **A** We're going on vacation next month.
   B Really? Where **are you going to go** / **are you going**?

7 **A** How do you get to work?
   B I usually catch the bus, but tomorrow **I'm going to drive** / **I'm driving** because the buses are on strike.

8 **A** Your sister drives too fast.
   B I know. I'm sure **she's going to have** / **she's having** an accident one day.

2 VOCABULARY verbs + prepositions

Complete the sentences with the correct prepositions.

1 I completely agree __*with*__ you.
2 We're arriving _____ Brazil at 6 a.m.
3 I'm worried _____ my flight because it's snowing.
4 They're waiting _____ Anna. She's late.
5 She spends a lot of money _____ clothes.
6 I want to speak _____ my boss after lunch.
7 Sarah's arriving _____ the airport tonight.
8 What do you think _____ the government's proposal?

3 PRONUNCIATION sounding friendly

a Number the dialogue in the correct order.

 1 Would you like to go away for the weekend?
 __ What about next weekend? What are you doing then?
 __ Are you free this weekend?
 __ I love it!
 __ OK. Let's go to the mountains – the scenery is beautiful!
 __ Sorry, no. I'm working on Saturday.
 __ Nothing. Next weekend is fine.
 __ I'd love to.
 __ Great. Do you like walking?

b **iChecker** Listen and check. Then listen again and repeat the sentences. Copy the rhythm.

19

4 READING

a Read the advertisement for a vacation. How many nights does the tour last?

Tour of the Magic Triangle: Prague – Vienna – Budapest

Visit these three beautiful capital cities and discover their historic monuments and lively atmosphere. Enjoy three wonderful cultural performances and return with unforgettable memories.

Prague

The tour starts in Prague, capital of the Czech Republic. A free bus takes you from the airport to your hotel, where you spend three nights. The price includes a tour of the city, a cruise on the Vltava River, a visit to a spa resort, and a performance at the Laterna Magika theater. From Prague you travel first class by train to your next destination: Vienna.

Vienna

The Austrian capital has many spectacular monuments, which you can visit with the free 72-hour travel card that you receive when you arrive in Vienna. The price also includes a tour of the city, Viennese coffee and cakes at the famous Hotel Sacher, and a performance at the opera. After your three nights in Vienna you travel first class by train to your final destination: Budapest.

Budapest

You spend your last three nights in Budapest, the capital city of Hungary, where there are plenty of places to explore. The city is divided into two parts: the old historic city of Buda on the hill, and the commercial city of Pest on the other side of the Danube River. The price includes a tour of the city with a visit to the Hungarian Parliament Building a typical Hungarian dinner, a performance of classical music, and the return trip from your hotel to the airport.

At only $1,999, this is an opportunity you cannot afford to miss!

b Read the advertisement again. Answer the questions with P (Prague), V (Vienna), or B (Budapest).

In which city do customers…?
1 travel free on public transportation _V_
2 have a traditional evening meal __
3 go on a boat trip __
4 listen to a concert __
5 have a drink and sweet snack __
6 go to a place to relax __

c Underline five words you don't know. Use your dictionary to look up their meaning and pronunciation.

USEFUL WORDS AND PHRASES

Learn these words and phrases.

(travel) arrangements /əˈreɪndʒmənts/	still /stɪl/
conference /ˈkɑnfrəns/	both of us /ˈboʊθ əv ʌs/
news /nuz/	I'd love to /aɪd ˈlʌv tu/
fix /fɪks/	for ages /fɔr ˈeɪdʒɪz/
perhaps /pərˈhæps/	How are things? /haʊ ər ˈθɪŋz/

5 LISTENING

a **iChecker** Listen to two people, Chris and Dawn, talking about a vacation train trip. Which country is Dawn visiting? Is she going to eat and sleep on the train?

_____

b **iChecker** Listen again and correct the sentences.
1 Dawn is taking a vacation train trip **on her own**.
   with a friend
2 Chris went on a train trip when he was **a child**.

   _____
3 Dawn is going on the train trip for **a month**.

   _____
4 Dawn's trip starts in **Los Mochis**.

   _____
5 Dawn wants to **go to stores** in Mazatlan.

   _____

What is a rebel? A man who says no.

Albert Camus, French writer

3C What's the word?

1 GRAMMAR defining relative clauses

a Match the beginnings and ends of the sentences.

1 That's the hotel ☐ *f*
2 I need a cellphone ☐
3 My mom is the only person ☐
4 I love the picture ☐
5 That bus is the one ☐
6 Indio is the Californian town ☐
7 David Hockney is the artist ☐
8 That's the restaurant ☐

a that has a good camera.
b that my brother takes to work.
c that serves fresh fish.
d who remembers my birthday.
e who painted *Mr. & Mrs. Clarke*.
f where we spent our honeymoon.
g where they have the Coachella Music Festival.
h that is on the wall of your room.

b Complete the sentences with *who*, *that*, or *where*.

1 Do you know the man __who__ lives next door?
2 That's the gallery _____ had the Leonardo da Vinci exhibition.
3 Are those the people _____ are selling their house?
4 Do you know a good restaurant _____ is open on Sunday night?
5 Is that the bus _____ goes to the airport?
6 We walked past the school _____ their children go.
7 She's the woman _____ everyone is talking about.
8 I took my laptop back to the store _____ I bought it.
9 Santiago is the city _____ I lived as a child.
10 Is there someone _____ can speak Arabic in your class?

2 VOCABULARY expressions for paraphrasing: *like, for example*, etc.

Complete the sentences for explaining words.

1 *cheap*   It's the o_opposite_ of *generous*.
2 *cardigan*   It's a k_____ of sweater.
3 *smart*   It's s_____ to *intelligent*.
4 *slim*   It's l_____ *thin*, but it's more polite.
5 *souvenir*   It's s_____ you buy to remind you of your vacation.
6 *sunbathe*   For e_____, you do this on the beach.
7 *pilot*   It's s_____ who flies a plane.
8 *campsite*   It's s_____ you can sleep in tents.

3 PRONUNCIATION pronunciation in a dictionary

a Match the words with their pronunciation. Use your dictionary.

1 beard   _b_   a /bɔld/
  bald   _a_   b /bɪrd/

2 quiet   __   a /kwaɪt/
  quite   __   b /ˈkwaɪət/

3 shoes   __   a /ʃuz/
  socks   __   b /sɑks/

4 suit   __   a /swit/
  sweet   __   b /sut/

5 sightsee __   a /ˈsaɪtsi/
  sunbathe __   b /ˈsʌnbeɪð/

6 height   __   a /weɪt/
  weight   __   b /haɪt/

7 shirt   __   a /ʃərt/
  shorts   __   b /ʃɔrts/

8 crowded __   a /ˈklaʊdi/
  cloudy   __   b /ˈkraʊdəd/

b 🔲 iChecker Listen and check. Then listen again and repeat the words.

4 READING

a Read the definitions and complete them with these words.

agritourism chick lit E-waste fashionista netiquette sandwich generation staycation ~~web rage~~

More new words in English

1 _Web rage_ is the angry feeling you get because of a problem with the Internet.

2 A _____ is a person who always wears the latest styles.

3 _____ is a kind of book that tells a story from a woman's point of view.

4 _____ is all the electrical machines and devices that people throw away.

5 The _____ is a group of people who take care of their parents at the same time as they're taking care of their children.

6 _____ is a kind of vacation where people stay on farms and help with all the work.

7 _____ is a set of rules that explains how to be polite on the Internet.

8 A _____ is a vacation that you spend at home.

b Underline five more words you don't know. Use your dictionary to look up their meaning and pronunciation.

5 LISTENING

a iChecker Listen to a radio program about the word game _Scrabble_. How many different names has the game had?

b iChecker Listen again. Mark the sentences T (true) or F (false).

1 Alfred Mosher Butts was out of work when he invented the game.   _T_

2 The game of _Lexico_ had a board and letter tiles.   ___

3 Butts used a newspaper to count the frequency of the letters in English.   ___

4 Butts gave the letters A, E, I, O, and U one point each.   ___

5 Butts gave 12 points to the most difficult letters to use.   ___

6 _Scrabble_ became popular in 1948.   ___

7 Butts and Brunot sold the rights to the game to another manufacturer.   ___

8 You can buy _Scrabble_ in more than a hundred different countries.   ___

1 VOCABULARY

Complete the sentences.

1 Can we have a t*able*___ for two, please?
2 What's on the m_____ today?
3 The st_____ is chicken soup or tomato salad.
4 I'll have the steak for my m_____ c_____.
5 Let's ask the w_____ for another bottle of water.
6 I don't want a d_____, but I'd like a coffee.
7 Can we have the c_____, please?

2 AT THE RESTAURANT

Order the dialogue.

A	Are you ready to order?	*1*
B	Still.	__
A	Still or sparkling?	__
B	Yes, please.	__
A	And how would you like your steak? Rare, medium, or well done?	__
B	A baked potato, please.	__
A	Can I get you something to start with?	__
B	Rare, please.	*6*
A	Here's your steak, ma'am.	__
B	Water, please.	__
A	Would you like that with fries or with a baked potato?	__
B	I'm sorry, but I asked for my steak rare and this is well done.	__
A	OK. And to drink?	__
B	No, thank you. Just a main course. I'd like the steak, please.	__
A	I'm very sorry, ma'am. I'll take it back to the kitchen.	*15*

3 SOCIAL ENGLISH

Complete the sentences with the words in the box.

a mistake	be great	my day	any suggestions
start with	~~tell me~~	to go	we have

1 A So, ___ *tell me* ___, Adam, what are your plans?
  B Well, to _____, I'd like to see the world.
2 A I'd like to go sightseeing this afternoon. Do you have _____?
  B How about going to Central Park? I could take you.
  A That would _____.
3 A Could _____ the check, please?
  B Yes, of course. Here you are.
4 A Excuse me. I think there's _____.
  B Oh, sorry. It's not _____ today.
5 A It's very late.
  B Yes. Time _____.

4 READING

a Read the article and answer the questions.

1 How many restaurants are there in New York? _Over 20,000_
2 What time do restaurants serve early-bird menus?
  _____
3 How much is the early-bird menu at Cucina di Pesce?
  _____
4 Where is La Paella? _____
5 Which restaurants serve a pre-theater dinner menu?
  _____
6 How much do they cost? _____
7 When is it cheapest to eat in a four-star restaurant?
  _____
8 What kind of food can you eat at Aquavit?
  _____

Eating out in NY

New York City has over 20,000 restaurants serving all kinds of food. However, eating out in the Big Apple can be very expensive. Here are some tips on how to save money during your stay.

Early-Bird Menus

These are meals served in some New York restaurants between 5 p.m. and 7 p.m., when they would normally be empty. If you don't mind having dinner early, you can enjoy a three-course meal for between $13 and $25.

Cucina di Pesce (87 E. 4th St.) serves great Italian food on its $12.95 early-bird menu. If you prefer something Spanish, you can try the $16.99 early-bird menu at **La Paella** (214 E. 9th St.).

Pre-Theater Dinner Menus

These are similar to early-bird menus, but they are served in the Theater District. Most of the restaurants here offer a special menu at a fixed price ranging from $30 to $45. The offer is only available before the show, and it starts at 5 p.m.

Four-Star Restaurants

These are all very expensive at dinnertime, so why not have lunch there instead? That way you can get dinner-quality food at lunchtime menu prices. **Aquavit** (65 E. 55th St.) serves fantastic Scandinavian food on a great lunch menu and **Jean Georges** (1 Central Park West) offers an excellent two-course lunch for only $28.

b <u>Underline</u> five words or phrases you don't know. Use your dictionary to look up their meaning and pronunciation.

Few things are more satisfying than seeing
your children have teenagers of their own.
Doug Larson, American journalist

4A Parents and teenagers

1 VOCABULARY housework, *make* or *do*?

a Complete the expressions with these verbs.

| clean   do   make   ~~pick up~~   put away   set   take out |

1 _pick up_____ dirty clothes
2 _____ the beds, lunch
3 _____ the table for dinner
4 _____ the floor, the bathroom
5 _____ the garbage
6 _____ the ironing, the dishes
7 _____ the clothes on your bed

b Complete the sentences with *do* or *make*.

1 He never forgets to __do__ his homework after school.
2 I try not to _____ a noise when I get up early.
3 My husband doesn't often _____ lunch.
4 I always _____ the crossword in the Sunday newspaper.
5 We always _____ housework on Saturday mornings.
6 Some children _____ friends easily when they go to school.
7 I love to _____ yoga, but I don't often have time for it.
8 Sorry, I need to _____ a phone call.

2 GRAMMAR present perfect + *yet* and *already*

a Add *already* or *yet* to these sentences in the correct place.

1 I've done the laundry.
   _I've already done the laundry_____.
2 Have you made any plans for the weekend?
   _____?
3 We haven't finished lunch.
   _____.
4 Daniel has cleaned his room.
   _____.
5 I've done the ironing.
   _____.
6 Have you been to the supermarket?
   _____?
7 I haven't cleaned the bathroom.
   _____.
8 Kenji has taken out the garbage.
   _____.

b Complete the sentences for each picture. Use the present perfect form of the verbs in parentheses.

1 She _has already done_ (already / do) the dishes.
2 He _____ (yet / not get up).
3 They _____ (already / win) the championship.
4 She _____ (yet / not clean the floor).
5 He _____ (already / set) the table.
6 "You're just in time. We _____ (yet / not eat)."

3 PRONUNCIATION /y/, /dʒ/

a Write a word containing the sound in the pictures.

1 a kind of exercise   _yoga_
2 the opposite of *old*   _____
3 twelve months   _____
4 a color   _____
5 special clothes for school _____

dʒ

6 a kind of short coat   _____
7 a person between 13 and
  19 years old   _____
8 something that helps people
  cross a river   _____
9 where professors teach   _____
10 get pleasure from something _____

b 🔊 iChecker Listen and check. Then listen again and repeat the words.

4 READING

a Read the text. Which is the best title?

1 **Having a cleaner house**
2 **Equality in the home**
3 **Improving your relationship**

Men and women all over the world have arguments about doing housework, and it's usually the women who lose. However, a study by researchers at the University of Michigan in the US shows that the situation is slowly improving.

The researchers asked 8,000 American families how much time they spent on housework each week. The researchers have asked the same 8,000 families the same questions every year since 1968. Then, each year, the researchers analyze the information.

The information showed that women in the US today spend about 16 hours a week doing housework. Men, on the other hand, spend about 12 hours a week doing the same things. Although women still spend more time doing domestic jobs, the figures show that the situation has improved. In the 1970s, women spent about 26 hours a week on housework and men only seven hours a week.

Researchers say that women are still doing most of the housework because people still divide domestic jobs into two areas. They see cooking, cleaning, and taking care of the children as "women's work," and general repairs, car maintenance, and work outside the home as "men's work."

So, in general, the results of the study bring good news for women. The difference between the amount of time men and women spend on housework is getting smaller every year. This means the time will come when both sexes share domestic chores equally. However, women will have to be extremely patient because the change won't be complete anytime soon!

b Read the text. Mark the sentences T (true) or F (false).

1 Men and women don't always agree about housework.   *T*
2 Different families answer the questions for the study each year.   __
3 The participants have answered the questions for 60 years.   __
4 The time people spend doing housework has changed since the 1970s.   __
5 Today, women do more housework than they did in the 1970s.   __
6 In general, people think it's normal for women to take care of the family car.   __
7 Next year, men and women will share the housework.   __

c Look at the highlighted words. What do you think they mean? Use your dictionary to look up their meaning and pronunciation.

5 LISTENING

a iChecker Listen to five teenagers talking about housework. Which speaker does the most housework?

_____

b iChecker Listen again. Match the speakers with what they say about housework.

Speaker 1   *B*   A We all share it.
Speaker 2   __   B My mom does it all.
Speaker 3   __   C We pay someone to do it.
Speaker 4   __   D There's one thing I like doing.
Speaker 5   __   E I do a little every day.

USEFUL WORDS AND PHRASES

Learn these words and phrases.

caregiver /ˈkɛrgɪvər/
plate /pleɪt/
reputation /rɛpyəˈteɪʃn/
teenager /ˈtineɪdʒər/
closet /ˈklɑzət/
dry (your hair) /draɪ/
knock (on the door) /nɑk/
keep on (texting) /kip ɑn/
turn off (your cell phone) /tərn ɑf/
TV channel /ti ˈvi ˈtʃænl/

4B Fashion and shopping

1 VOCABULARY shopping

a Complete the text.

SHOPPING IN A SHOP OR STORE

I usually go shopping during my lunch break, so I don't have time to [1]try__ on clothes. There's always a long line for the [2]f_____ r_____, so I just take them straight to the [3]ch_____ to pay. I keep the [4]r_____ so I can exchange them if they don't [5]s_____ me. Sometimes I get the wrong [6]s_____, and the clothes don't [7]f_____. I often [8]t_____ things b_____ to stores, but the [9]s_____ don't seem to mind at all.

b Complete the crossword.

				[1]A
	[2]			C
[3]				C
				O
[4] [5]				U
				N
[6]				T
[7]				
[8]					

Shopping online

Clues down ↓
1 When you shop online, you usually have to create an a*ccount* that has your personal information.
2 Something you want to buy is called an it_____.
5 eBay is an online au_____ site that sells things to the person who offers the most money.
7 Amazon is a popular w_____ where you can buy things such as books, computers, and clothes.

Clues across →
3 When you find something you want to buy on a website, you put it in your shopping c_____.
4 You can make a p_____ in different ways, e.g., using your credit card or Paypal.
6 When you are ready to buy something, you go to the ch_____.
8 You have to enter your d_____ address so they can send your things to the correct place.

2 GRAMMAR present perfect or simple past?

a Write sentences and questions with the present perfect. Use contractions where possible.

1 she / buy / a new jacket [+]
She's bought a new jacket.
2 I / bring / my / credit card [−]
_______________.
3 Anna / go shopping [?]
_______________?
4 your sister / ever work / as a model [?]
_______________?
5 you / wear / your new shirt [−]
_______________.
6 I / ever tell you/ about my vacation in Thailand [?]
_______________?
7 the mall / never be / so crowded [+]
_______________.
8 I / never use / eBay [+]
_______________.

b Complete the dialogues. Use the present perfect or simple past.

1 **A** *Have you ever bought* (you / ever / buy) any clothes on the Internet?
B Yes, I *have*.
A What *did you buy* (you / buy)?
B I *bought* (buy) a dress for a wedding, but it didn't fit!

2 **A** __________ (you / ever / sell) anything on eBay?
B Yes, I __________.
A What __________ (you / sell)?
B Some CDs. I __________ (not want) them anymore.

3 **A** __________ (you / ever / wear) any expensive jewelry?
B No, I __________.

4 **A** __________ (you / ever / lose) your wallet?
B Yes, I __________. I __________ (leave) it in a cart at the supermarket.

5 **A** __________ (you / ever / have) an argument with a salesperson?
B Yes, I __________. I __________ (not have) the receipt, so I __________ (not can) exchange a pair of boots.

3 PRONUNCIATION *c* and *ch*

a iChecker Listen and circle the word with a different sound.

key	1	customer	account	(choose)
key	2	click	proceed	chemistry
snake	3	clothes	city	receipt
snake	4	receive	card	nice

b iChecker Listen again and repeat the words.

4 LISTENING

a iChecker Listen to a news story. What is Westfield?
_______________.

b iChecker Listen again and answer the questions.

1 How long has it taken to build Westfield?
Six years.
2 How much did the shopping mall cost?
_______________.
3 How many department stores and small stores are there?
_______________.
4 How many cafes and restaurants are there?
_______________.
5 How many people work at Westfield?
_______________.
6 How can you get to Westfield?
_______________.
7 What did the reporter want to buy?
_______________.
8 Why didn't the reporter buy the thing she liked?
_______________.

USEFUL WORDS AND PHRASES

Learn these words and phrases.

bride /braɪd/
bridegroom /ˈbraɪdgrum/
leather /ˈlɛðər/
sew /soʊ/
bare feet /bɛr fit/
costume /ˈkɑstum/
fashion designer /ˈfæʃn dɪˈzaɪnər/
high heels /ˈhaɪ hilz/
wedding dress /ˈwɛdɪŋ drɛs/
take off (your shoes) /teɪk ɑf/

4C Lost weekend

1 GRAMMAR *something, anything, nothing, etc.*

a (Circle) the correct word.

1 We didn't do (**anything**) / **nothing** special last weekend.
2 Do you know **anything** / **anyone** about the meeting today?
3 There isn't **anywhere** / **nowhere** to go in the evenings.
4 He couldn't find his keys **nowhere** / **anywhere**.
5 We didn't know **someone** / **anyone** at the party.
6 Daniel has **something** / **anything** to tell you.
7 I called you twice, but **anybody** / **nobody** answered.
8 We need to find **somewhere** / **anywhere** to stay in Toronto.
9 Listen! I think **somebody** / **anybody** is upstairs.

b Look at the picture. Mark the sentences T (true) or F (false).

1 There isn't anywhere to sit.   *F*
2 The man on the right is eating something.   —
3 Nobody is dancing.   —
4 There's nothing on the ground.   —
5 Someone is playing with the dog.   —
6 The man cooking doesn't have anything on his head. —
7 There isn't anybody in the swimming pool.   —

2 VOCABULARY adjectives ending in *-ed* and *-ing*

Complete the sentences with an adjective ending in *-e* or *-ing*.

1 I'm reading a really in*teresting* book.
2 Going to a spa for the weekend is so r_____.
3 This movie is really b_____. Turn the TV off.
4 Helen's very d_____. She's just lost her job.
5 My cousin is very in_____ in archaeology.
6 Congratulations! That's really ex_____ news.
7 The news right now is all very d_____.
8 We always feel very r_____ on vacation.
9 Mom, I'm b_____! I don't have anything to do!
10 The dogs were very ex_____ to see us when we came home.

3 PRONUNCIATION /ɛ/, /oʊ/, /ʌ/

a iChecker Listen and write the words in the chart.

a̶n̶y̶t̶h̶i̶n̶g̶   c̶l̶o̶t̶h̶e̶s̶   c**oa**t   c̶u̶s̶t̶o̶m̶e̶r̶
d**o**n't   dr**e**ss   fr**ie**ndly   f**u**nny   gl**o**ves
g**o**es   h**o**me   l**u**nch   n**e**ver   n**o**thing   ph**o**tos
s**o**mething   sw**ea**ter   w**e**bsite

1 ɛ egg	2 oʊ phone	3 ʌ up
anything	*clothes*	*customer*

b iChecker Listen and check. Then listen again and repeat the words.

4 READING

a Complete the text with the activities.

Bake a loaf of bread	Organize your shelves
Clean your closet	Play board games
Listen to some podcasts	Start a blog
Learn how to juggle	Take some photos
Meet your neighbors	~~Visit a library~~

Ten free things to do on the weekend

The weekend is the time when most people spend the most money. Here are some activities you can do if you want to save money.

1 ___Visit a library___. It doesn't cost anything to borrow a book, and there may be some DVDs you want to watch.

2 _____. Throw away any clothes you never wear, or give them to a charity.

3 _____. Many websites have interesting interviews you can listen to for free.

4 _____. This is a great way to spend time with the whole family.

5 _____. You probably have the ingredients in a cupboard – the result is delicious!

6 _____. All you need is three balls and a video showing you how to do it.

7 _____. Invite them over for a coffee and a chat and get to know them better.

8 _____. Decide which books, CDs, and DVDs you want to keep and get rid of the rest.

9 _____. Go for a walk with your digital camera. You'll be surprised at how beautiful your city is.

10 _____. Not only is it fun, but writing improves your communication skills.

b <u>Underline</u> five words you don't know. Use your dictionary to look up their meaning and pronunciation.

5 LISTENING

a 〔iChecker〕 Listen to four people talking about their weekends. Where did they go?

Speaker 1 _____
Speaker 2 _____
Speaker 3 _____
Speaker 4 _____

b 〔iChecker〕 Listen again. Which speaker…?

1 cooked a meal ___
2 played with children ___
3 went to a different country ___
4 saw some interesting exhibitions ___
5 had an argument *1*
6 woke up early ___
7 had bad weather *1*
8 gave someone a surprise ___

USEFUL WORDS AND PHRASES

Learn these words and phrases.

survey /ˈsərveɪ/
encourage /ɪnˈkərɪdʒ/
impress /ɪmˈprɛs/
invent /ɪnˈvɛnt/
lie (about something) /laɪ/
lie down /laɪ ˈdaʊn/
do paperwork /du ˈpeɪpərwərk/
press (the button) /prɛs/
tell the truth /tɛl ðə ˈtruθ/
elevator button /ˈɛləveɪtər bʌtn/

〔iChecker〕 〔TESTS〕 FILE 4

Time is the coin of your life. You spend it.
Do not allow others to spend it for you.

Carl Sandburg, American poet

5A No time for anything

1 GRAMMAR comparative adjectives and adverbs, *as...as*

a Complete the sentences with the correct comparative form of the adjective / adverb.

1 My new boss is __*more patient*__ than my old one. (patient)
2 Pollution is _____ in cities than it is in the country. (bad)
3 We aren't in a hurry. You can drive _____. (slowly)
4 The summers here are _____ than they were in the past. (hot)
5 I failed the test. I'll work _____ next time. (hard)
6 It's _____ to my parents' house than it is to my best friend's. (far)
7 You can make the dinner tonight. You cook _____ than me. (good)
8 The Japanese diet is _____ than the American diet. (healthy)
9 A motorcycle is _____ than a car. (dangerous)
10 Los Angeles International Airport is _____ than San Francisco International Airport. (busy)

b Rewrite the sentences using *as...as*.

1 This car goes faster than that one.
That car doesn't *go as fast as this one* _____.
2 Her shoes were more stylish than her handbag.
Her handbag wasn't _____.
3 My boss's office is bigger than mine.
My office isn't _____.
4 South Korea played better than the US.
The US didn't _____.
5 I drive more carefully than you.
You don't _____.
6 Laptops are more expensive than cell phones.
Cell phones aren't _____.
7 Ben looks more relaxed than Anna.
Anna doesn't _____.
8 His shirt was dirtier than his pants.
His pants weren't _____.

2 VOCABULARY time expressions

Complete the sentences with a word from the box.

in	on	save	spend	~~take~~	waste

1 The flight to Beijing is going to __*take*__ about 11 hours.
2 She needs to _____ more time studying.
3 I hope we arrive _____ time. My dad is meeting me at the airport.
4 Don't _____ time doing things you don't enjoy.
5 We'll _____ time if we go on the freeway. There's much less traffic.
6 My wife gets very stressed when she's _____ a hurry.

3 PRONUNCIATION word stress

a Underline the stressed syllable in these words.

1 di|et
2 dan|ge|rous
3 par|ents
4 a|go
5 chil|dren
6 a|bove
7 prob|lem
8 co|mmu|ni|ca|tion
9 tra|di|tion|al
10 a|round
11 se|conds
12 fa|mous

b Now (circle) the /ə/ sound in the words above.

1 di(et)

c **iChecker** Listen and check. Then listen again and repeat the words.

4 READING

a Read the story.

The fisherman and the banker

A banker was on vacation abroad. He was walking on a beautiful beach near a small town. He saw a fisherman in his boat with a few fish in it.

"Great fish!" he said. "How long did it take you to catch them?"

"Not very long," answered the fisherman.

"Why didn't you stay in the ocean longer to catch some more?" asked the banker.

"There are just enough fish here to feed my family," answered the fisherman.

Then the banker asked, "But what do you do the rest of the time?"

"I sleep late, I fish a little, I play with my kids, and I relax. In the evening, I go to see my friends in the town. We play the guitar. I'm busier than you think. Life here isn't as…"

The banker interrupted him. "I have an MBA from Harvard University, and I can help you. You're not fishing as much as you can. If you start fishing for longer periods of time, you'll get enough money from selling the fish to buy a bigger boat. Then with the money you'll get from catching and selling more fish, you could buy a second boat, and then a third one, and so on. Then instead of selling your fish to stores, you could sell them directly to a fish factory, or even open your own factory. Then you'll be able to leave your little town for the city, and finally move to New York City, where you could run the company."

"How long will that take?" asked the fisherman.

"About 15 to 20 years," answered the banker.

"And then?"

"Then it gets more interesting," said the banker, smiling and talking more quickly. "When the moment comes, you can put your company on the stock market, and you will make millions."

"Millions? But then what?"

"Then you can retire, live in a small town by the ocean, go to the beach, sleep late, play with your kids…"

b Mark the sentences T (true) or F (false).

1 The fisherman needed to catch more fish.   *F*
2 The banker thought he was very busy.   ___
3 The banker wanted him to work harder.   ___
4 He told the fisherman to buy more boats.   ___
5 The banker said that he couldn't live in New York City.   ___
6 The banker promised the fisherman a lot of money.   ___

5 LISTENING

a **iChecker** Listen to five speakers talk about how their lives have changed. Who…?

1 has just started working from home   ___
2 has had a baby   ___
3 has lost his / her job   ___
4 has moved to a different country   *1*
5 has retired   ___

b **iChecker** Listen again. Which two people are happiest about the changes?

_____
_____

Who is the least happy?

_____

USEFUL WORDS AND PHRASES

Learn these words and phrases.

abbreviations /əˌbriviˈeɪʃnz/
characters /ˈkærəktərz/
nowadays /ˈnaʊədeɪz/
story /ˈstɔri/
irritable /ˈɪrətəbl/
patient (opp *impatient*) /ˈpeɪʃnt/
line /laɪn/
stressed /strɛst/
stressful /ˈstrɛsfl/
tips /tɪps/

5B Superlative cities

1 GRAMMAR superlatives
(+ *ever* + present perfect)

a Complete the sentences with the superlative of an adjective from the box.

bad	exciting	far	friendly
good	safe	ugly	wet

1 The traffic is awful in the middle of the city. The ___best___ way to travel around is by the subway.
2 It rains a lot here in the spring. The _____ month is April.
3 The _____ I've ever driven is from Boston to Chicago. It took me 16 hours.
4 It was the _____ hotel I've ever stayed in. The service was awful, so we only spent one night there.
5 The _____ buildings are in the new part of the city. They really aren't nice to look at.
6 The streets are very dangerous at night. The _____ place to be is in the hotel.
7 The _____ part of our tour was in Rio de Janeiro. We saw the first day of the carnival.
8 The _____ city I've ever visited is Vancouver. I found the people very helpful.

b Circle the correct word or phrase.

1 That hotel has the **dirtier** / **dirtiest** rooms I have ever seen.
2 It's **the most interesting** / **more interesting** museum in Miami.
3 This is the **more expensive** / **most expensive** souvenir I've ever bought.
4 That restaurant serves the **better** / **best** pasta we've ever eaten.
5 The summer is the **busyest** / **busiest** time of year.

c Write sentences with *ever*.

1 He / rude waiter / I / meet
   He's the rudest waiter I've ever met .
2 That / fast car / I / drive
   _____ .
3 It / beautiful building / we / see
   _____ .
4 That / healthy meal / he / eat
   _____ .
5 It / good photograph / you / take
   _____ .
6 This / exciting sport / I / play
   _____ .
7 That / bad flight / we / have
   _____ .
8 This / interesting city / I / visit
   _____ .

2 VOCABULARY describing a town or city

a Complete the description of Santa Barbara.

Santa Barbara is a city about 90 miles [1]n___orth___ of Los Angeles, California on the [2]c_____ of the Pacific Ocean. It is [3]w_____ of the Santa Ynez Mountains. It has a [4]p_____ of about 88,000 people and is [5]f_____ as an ocean-side resort.

b Complete the sentences with the opposite of the adjectives in parentheses.

1 Some of the buildings in the city are very m_odern_. (old)

2 Los Angeles is a very p_____ city – there are so many cars. (clean)

3 New York City is a very s_____ city these days. (dangerous)

4 Mumbai is an extremely n_____ city. (quiet)

5 Where's the most b_____ place you've ever been to? (interesting)

6 The subway in Tokyo is very c_____. (empty)

c (Circle) the different word.

1	cathedral	church	(shopping mall)
2	mosque	temple	town hall
3	market	castle	department store
4	statue	palace	museum

3 PRONUNCIATION word stress

a **iChecker** Listen and <u>under</u>line the stressed syllable.

1 beau|ti|ful
2 crowd|ed
3 dir|ty
4 ex|ci|ting
5 fright|en|ing
6 ge|ne|rous
7 in|te|res|ting
8 po|llu|ted
9 ro|man|tic

b **iChecker** Listen again and repeat the words.

4 LISTENING

a **iChecker** Listen to a radio travel program about Brazil. Check (✓) the places that are mentioned in the program.

1 Búzios ✓ 4 Rio de Janeiro ☐
2 Salvador ☐ 5 São Paulo ☐
3 Brasília ☐ 6 Recife ☐

b **iChecker** Listen again and answer T (true) or F (false).

1 Salvador is an old city. _T_
2 Eight million people live in Rio de Janeiro. __
3 The churches in Rio de Janeiro are all very new. __
4 You can take a bus to visit the peninsula. __
5 The best time to visit is December to March. __

USEFUL WORDS AND PHRASES

Learn these words and phrases.

architecture /ˈɑrkətɛktʃər/
culture /ˈkʌltʃər/
inhabitants /ɪnˈhæbətənts/
without /wɪˈðaʊt/
nightlife /ˈnaɪtlaɪf/
several /ˈsɛvrəl/
foreign /ˈfɔrən/
romantic /roʊˈmæntɪk/
rude /rud/
pretend (to do something) /prɪˈtɛnd/

I've been on a diet for two weeks,
and all I've lost is fourteen days.

Totie Fields, American actress

5C How much is too much?

1 VOCABULARY health and the body

Complete the sentences with these words.

~~anxious~~ bones brain faces illness prevent skin

1 I'm ___anxious___ about my uncle's health because he's been sick for a long time.
2 People suffering from a serious _____ often stay in the hospital for a long time.
3 You need to cover your _____ with sunscreen when you sunbathe.
4 You can tell they've been in the sun – their _____ are very red.
5 When you're old, your _____ can break more easily.
6 Coffee can sometimes _____ you from sleeping.
7 My grandmother can't move very well, but her _____ is still active.

2 GRAMMAR quantifiers, *too, not enough*

a Complete the sentences with *a few, a little, much, enough, many,* or *a lot of.*

1 She's overweight because she eats ___a lot of___ unhealthy food.
2 Can I ask you _____ questions about your diet? It won't take long.
3 Her children don't have healthy diets – they don't eat _____ vegetables.
4 How _____ sugar do you put in your coffee?
5 Could I have _____ more tea, please?
6 I don't eat _____ fruit – I need to eat more.
7 How _____ hours do you spend in front of the TV every day?
8 _____ time in the sun is good for you, but no more than 15 minutes.
9 He's in his last year of school, so he gets _____ homework.
10 I only drink _____ cups of coffee a day – maybe two or three.

b Circle the correct phrase.

1 I can't go to the party. I'm **too** / **too much** sick.
2 I'm not very good at basketball. I'm not **enough tall** / **tall enough**.
3 I couldn't live in Florida. It rains **too many** / **too much**.
4 I'm not going to finish my homework. I don't have **enough time** / **time enough**.
5 I can't sleep. I've eaten **too much** / **too many** chocolate.
6 I can't carry my groceries home. I have **too much** / **too many** bags.
7 I'm really out of shape. I don't **enough exercise** / **exercise enough**.
8 I'm always tired. I don't **enough sleep** / **sleep enough**.

3 PRONUNCIATION /ʌ/, /u/, /aɪ/, /ɛ/

a **iChecker** Listen and write the words in the chart.

any	diet	~~enough~~	few	food	healthy
like	many	much	none	time	too

1 **ʌ** up	*enough*	
2 **u** boot		
3 **aɪ** bike		
4 **ɛ** egg		

b **iChecker** Listen and check. Then listen again and repeat the words.

4 READING

a Read the newspaper article. Which one of these fruits and vegetables do not count toward your five a day?

beans ☐   potatoes ☐
peaches ☐   cucumbers ☐
carrots ☐   peas ☐
plums ☐   pineapples ☐

b Read the article again and write T (true) or F (false).

1 The campaign to eat more healthy food in the US is called Fruits & Veggies—More Servings.   _F_
2 Fruit in a can isn't good for you.   __
3 Frozen vegetables don't count toward your five a day.   __
4 Only 100-percent pure fruit juice counts as a serving.   __
5 One mandarin orange counts as one serving.   __
6 You have to eat many tomatoes to get one serving.   __
7 A large spoonful of vegetables doesn't count as a serving.   __

c Look at the highlighted words. What do you think they mean? Check with your dictionary.

5 LISTENING

a iChecker Listen to two people taking a quiz about body age. How old is Alice? What is her body age?

b iChecker Listen again and complete the sentences.

1 Alice walks ___a lot___ every day.
2 She plays _____ sports.
3 She doesn't eat _____ fast food.
4 She eats _____ fruits and vegetables.
5 She's a very _____ person.
6 She's _____ stressed.
7 She sees _____ close friends regularly.
8 She doesn't have _____ time for herself.

USEFUL WORDS AND PHRASES

Learn these words and phrases.

bones /boʊnz/   skills /skɪlz/
brain /breɪn/   skin /skɪn/
face /feɪs/   sunlight /ˈsʌnlaɪt/
illness /ˈɪlnəs/   sunscreen /ˈsʌnskrin/
prevent /prɪˈvɛnt/   anxious /ˈæŋkʃəs/

iChecker TESTS FILE 5

Fruits & Veggies—More Matters

How much fruit do you eat every day? And how many vegetables? Food experts today think that we don't have enough of these foods in our diet, and they say that we eat too much fat and sugar. This is why the World Health Organization has started a campaign to encourage us to eat more fruits and vegetables. The campaign in the US is called Fruits & Veggies—More Matters.

Why eat fruits and vegetables?

Fruits and vegetables are full of important vitamins and minerals that our bodies need to be healthy. Scientific studies have shown that eating a lot of them can prevent some illnesses like diabetes and obesity. Also, fruits and vegetables don't contain much fat, and they don't have many calories, so they help us to keep thin.

What counts?

Almost all fruits and vegetables count toward your five a day, except potatoes. The food can be fresh, frozen, or in a can, like peaches or peas. It can be raw, cooked, or even dried, like raisins or banana chips. A glass of 100-percent fruit juice with no added sugar also counts as one serving.

How much is a serving?

A serving of fresh fruit or vegetables depends on the size of the food. In the case of small-sized fruit like plums or mandarin oranges, one serving is two pieces of fruit. A piece of medium-sized fruit like an apple, an orange, or a pear also counts as one serving. With larger fruit like melon and pineapple, one serving is a one-half cup or about 3 ounces. We use the same method for calculating servings with vegetables. In the case of salad vegetables, a medium-sized tomato or 3.5-inch piece of cucumber count as one serving each. For smaller, cooked vegetables like beans and carrots, one serving is three large spoonfuls of vegetables.

1 VOCABULARY shopping

Match the prices.

1	79¢	c	a	fifty-nine pence
2	€30.49	☐	b	thirteen pounds ninety-nine
3	$3.89	☐	c	seventy-nine cents
4	59p	☐	d	thirty euros forty-nine
5	£13.99	☐	e	three dollars and eighty-nine cents

2 TAKING SOMETHING BACK TO A STORE

Complete the dialogue.

A Can I help you, [1]m*a'am*?

B Yes, I [2]b_____ this sweater yesterday.

A Yes, I remember. Is there a [3]pr_____?

B Yes, I'm [4]af_____ it's too small.

A What [5]s_____ is it?

B It's a [6]s_____. Do you have a [7]m_____?

A I'll go and [8]ch_____. Just a minute. I'm [9]s_____, but we don't have this sweater in your size. But we do have this one, and it's the same price. Or you can have a [10]r_____.

B Um...I'll take this one then, please. Can I try it on?

A Yes, of course. The [11]f_____ r_____ are over there. Is everything OK?

B Yes, this one fits perfectly.

A Good. Do you have the [12]r_____ for the other sweater?

B Yes, here you are.

3 SOCIAL ENGLISH

Order the dialogue.

A	Have you had a good day?	*1*
B	OK. When?	___
A	OK. See you later.	___
B	Can we make it a bit earlier? Say, seven thirty?	___
A	Why don't we go out for dinner? I know a great Italian restaurant.	___
A	Eight o'clock?	___
B	Oh, you know. Working! But it was OK.	___

4 READING

a Read the text. Where could you…?

1	make a toy	*FAO Schwarz*
2	try on a designer bracelet	_____
3	buy something for when you take a shower	_____
4	get a temporary tattoo	_____

Fifth Avenue Shopping

Fifth Avenue is one of the most expensive shopping streets in the world. Most of the world's luxury boutiques are located here, including Gucci, Prada, Armani, and Cartier. It is also home to huge department stores like Lord & Taylor, Barneys, and Bergdorf Goodman. Most stores are open daily from 10 a.m. to 7 p.m., and start later on Sundays. Here are some of the most well known:

FAO SCHWARZ

This world-famous toy store is popular with tourists and New Yorkers. The amazing Grand Hall has more than 20,000 colored lights. There's also a giant dance-on piano keyboard and an enormous candy store. Big kids can have a lot of fun in the do-it-yourself department, where they can even design their own doll.

RICKY'S

This ultra-fashionable beauty store has been selling the latest cosmetics, hair, and bath products for nearly two decades. Products range from the most expensive to the most ecological, so there's something for everybody. Upstairs, check out the fun clothing and accessories. You can also get temporary henna tattoos.

TIFFANY & CO.

This exclusive jewelry store has occupied its current location since 1940. Customers can admire the designer jewelry on the first floor before taking the elevator upstairs to choose an engagement ring. You can buy an elegant table, glass, and silverware on the fourth floor, and there are less pricey items on the third floor.

b Read the text again. Match the highlighted words to their meaning.

1	the set of keys on a piano	_____
2	very expensive	_____
3	scarves, belts, gloves, etc.	_____
4	an agreement to get married	_____
5	very big	_____
6	the activity of making things on your own	_____

A pessimist is someone who is pleased with bad experiences because they show he was right.

Heinz Ruhmann, German actor and movie director

6A Are you a pessimist?

1 GRAMMAR *will / won't* (predictions)

Complete the dialogues with *will / won't* and a verb from the list. Use contractions.

not remember   ~~fall~~   not sell   forget   not win   miss

1

A I'm going climbing next weekend.
B It's very dangerous. You *'ll fall* _____.

2

A I'm playing in the tennis final tomorrow.
B The other player is very good. You _____.

3

A I'm going to study all evening.
B It's a waste of time. You _____ anything in the morning.

4

A I told Nick that it's Jane's birthday on Friday.
B You know Nick! He _____.

5

A I'm going to put my MP3 player on eBay.
B It's too old. You _____ it.

6

A I'm taking the 8:50 train.
B It's leaving in five minutes. You _____ it.

2 VOCABULARY opposite verbs

Write the opposite verb in each space. Be careful – use the correct verb form.

1 **arrive**
You won't ___*leave*___ on time.

2 **teach**
We're going to _____ English in Canada.

3 **fail**
I don't think he _____ all of his exams.

4 **Push**
_____ the door to open it.

5 **fix**
I've _____ my glasses.

6 **lend**
Can I _____ a pen, please?

7 **win**
I think he's going to _____ the race.

8 **turn off**
Can you _____ the light, please?

9 **get**
I _____ more than 50 emails yesterday.

10 **lose**
I've _____ some money!

3 PRONUNCIATION *'ll, won't*

iChecker Listen and repeat. Copy the <u>rhy</u>thm.

1 I'll **learn a lot**.
2 He'll **meet** somebody **new**.
3 **You'll** have a **good time**.
4 She **won't** get the **job**.
5 They **won't lend** you the **money**.
6 We **won't <u>arrive</u>** on **time**.

4 READING

a Read the horoscopes for this month. Answer the questions.

Horoscopes

 AQUARIUS Jan 21–Feb 19
You'll find love this month! You'll meet someone new at work, which will be the start of something special. The color red will bring you happiness.

 PISCES Feb 20–Mar 20
Close family will be important this month. Try to spend more time with them, and they'll be very glad to see you. The color green will bring you money.

 ARIES Mar 21–Apr 20
You'll have to be very careful with money this month and avoid buying any clothes. However, you'll get a nice surprise at the end of the month. The color blue will bring you a surprise.

 TAURUS Apr 21–May 21
You'll have a very busy social life this month! Your friends will be taking you out all the time, and you'll make many new ones, too. The color orange will bring you success.

 GEMINI May 22–June 21
You won't have a very good month at work. Your boss will give you some bad news, but don't worry: you won't be unemployed. Work hard and next month will be better. The color purple will be important.

 CANCER June 22–July 22
This will be a great month for going away! You'll win a vacation, so have your passport ready. You'll also travel a lot in your own country, and you'll visit some old friends. The color yellow will bring you a fun surprise.

1 Who will do a lot of traveling this month?   *Cancer*
2 Who will have problems with their job?   _____
3 Who won't go shopping?   _____
4 Whose color will bring happiness?   _____
5 Who will go out a lot this month?   _____

b <u>Underline</u> five words you don't know. Use your dictionary to look up their meaning and pronunciation.

5 LISTENING

a **iChecker** Listen to a conversation about horoscopes. What are Matt and Amy's signs?

b **iChecker** Listen again and complete the sentences with A (Amy) or M (Matt).

1 __*A*__ believes in horoscopes.
2 _____ doesn't believe in horoscopes.
3 _____ has a problem with someone.
4 _____ is worried about the horoscope.
5 _____ was born in January.
6 _____'s horoscope is good.
7 _____ has a meeting the next day.

USEFUL WORDS AND PHRASES

Learn these words and phrases.

optimist /ˈɑptəmɪst/
pessimist /ˈpɛsəmɪst/
(TV) series /ˈsɪriz/
stranger /ˈstreɪndʒər/
cheer up /ˈtʃɪr ʌp/
definitely (not) /ˈdɛfənətli/
probably (not) /ˈprɑbəbli/
I doubt it. /aɪ ˈdaʊt ɪt/
I hope so. (opp *I hope not*) /aɪ ˈhoʊp soʊ/
I think so (opp *I don't think so*) /aɪ ˈθɪŋk soʊ/

Vote for the man who promises least;
he'll be the least disappointing.

Bernard Baruch, American political adviser

6B I'll never forget you

1 GRAMMAR *will / won't* (decisions, offers, promises)

a Write sentences using the pictures and prompts. Use *I'll / I won't*.

1 call / you tomorrow

   I'll call you tomorrow   .

2 lend / you some money

   _____.

3 have / the chicken

   _____.

4 take / your coat

   _____.

5 turn off / air-conditioning

   _____.

6 not / be late

   _____.

b Are these sentences promises (P), decisions (D), or offers (O)?

1 I'll drive you home.   *O*
2 I'll remember to tell her.   __
3 I'll get you some water.   __
4 I'll help you clean your room, if you like. __
5 I'll have the chocolate cake, please.   __
6 I won't tell your parents.   __

2 VOCABULARY verb + *back*

Complete the sentences with these verbs.

| ~~call~~ | come | give | pay | send | take |

1 A Jack called while you were out.
  B Thanks. I'll ___*call*___ him back in a minute.

2 A Do you want to borrow some money?
  B Yes, please. I'll _____ you back next week.

3 A The person you want to see isn't here. She's at lunch.
  B That's OK. I'll _____ back later.

4 A It's a really nice top, but it doesn't fit me.
  B Don't worry. I'll _____ it back to the store
    and exchange it.

5 A Have you finished that book I lent you?
  B Yes. I'll _____ it back to you tomorrow.

6 A That toy car you bought on the Internet doesn't work.
  B It doesn't? I'll _____ it back, then.

3 PRONUNCIATION word stress: two-syllable verbs

a **iChecker** Listen and underline the stressed syllables. Circle the words that are stressed on the second syllable.

1 worr|y   re|lax   be|come
2 de|cide   e|mail   pro|mise
3 prac|tice   li|sten   re|pair
4 borr|ow   for|get   a|gree
5 sun|bathe   in|vite   com|plain

b **iChecker** Listen and check. Then listen again and repeat the words.

4 **READING**

a Read the text. What did Paul learn from his experience?

An expensive lesson

My name's Paul, and this happened to me when I was visiting a friend in Paris.

I was getting off the Eurostar train at the Gare du Nord station when a man came up to me. He was wearing a suit, and he looked very respectable. "Do you speak English?" he asked. He had a French accent, but he said he was a banker from Montreal in the French-speaking part of Canada. Then he told me he had a problem. "I'm here in Paris with my wife and our three children, and we don't have enough money for a hotel. You see, my wife tried to get money from an ATM machine, but she couldn't remember our PIN number. She used the wrong number three times, so the machine kept her card. Could you help me?" I wasn't sure, so I asked to see his passport. "My passport is with my wife. She's waiting in a cafe with the children. We only need $100 for the night, and I promise I'll pay you back." By this time the man was actually crying, so I thought he was telling the truth. I agreed to lend him the money, and I wrote down his name, email address, and phone number in Montreal. Then we went to an ATM, and I gave him the money. He said thank you, gave me a big hug, and left. I never saw him or heard from him ever again.

I knew his story wasn't completely true. Why did a banker have only one bank card? Why didn't he tell me how he would pay me back? Were his wife and children really in the cafe, and did they even exist? But I was tired and in a foreign country, and I felt like I had to help him. I now know to be very careful who I talk to when I arrive somewhere new!

b Read the text. Number the sentences in the right order.

  a Paul wrote down the man's contact information. __

  b The man explained his problem. __

  c The man's wife had his passport. __

  d Paul arrived in Paris. _1_

  e Paul asked for the man's passport. __

  f A man started talking to him. __

  g Paul didn't hear from the man. __

  h Paul gave the man some money. __

c <u>Underline</u> five words you don't know. Use your dictionary to look up their meaning and pronunciation.

5 **LISTENING**

a **iChecker** Listen to five speakers describing problems they have had abroad. What do the speakers have in common?

b **iChecker** Listen again and match the speakers with the sentences.

Speaker 1   _D_

Speaker 2   __

Speaker 3   __

Speaker 4   __

Speaker 5   __

A Next time, I'll check before I go.
B I'll buy my own in the future.
C I won't let anyone in another time.
~~D I won't do anyone any favors in the future.~~
E I won't go out with anyone I don't know again.

USEFUL WORDS AND PHRASES

Learn these words and phrases.

hurt /hərt/
previous /ˈpriviəs/
relationship /rɪˈleɪʃnʃɪp/
extra-large order /ˈɛkstrə lɑrdʒ ˈɔrdər/
ice cream sundae /aɪs krim ˈsʌndeɪ/
get engaged /gɛt ɪnˈgeɪdʒd/
get in touch /gɛt ɪn ˈtʌtʃ/
in their twenties /ɪn ðər ˈtwɛntiz/

Only in our dreams are we free.
The rest of the time we need wages.

Terry Pratchett, British writer

6C The meaning of dreaming

1 GRAMMAR review of verb forms: present, past, and future

a Complete the dialogues with the correct form of the verbs in parentheses. Use contractions where possible.

1 **A** *Are* you *going to go out* tonight? (go out)
  B No, I'm really tired. I'm ___*going to go*___ to bed early. (go)

2 **A** What time _____ you usually _____ to bed? (go)
  B At 10:30. Then I _____ for an hour before I go to sleep. (read)

3 **A** Do you think the US _____ tonight? (win)
  B No, I think they _____. (lose)

4 **A** What _____ you _____ at midnight last night? (do)
  B I _____ TV. (watch)

5 **A** _____ you ever _____ that you were flying? (dream)
  B No, I _____ never _____ that dream. (have)

6 **A** What _____ you _____? It's 5 o'clock in the morning! (do)
  B I can't sleep so I _____. (read)

7 **A** _____ you _____ well last night? (sleep)
  B No, I _____ in the middle of the night, and I couldn't go back to sleep. (wake up)

8 **A** What time _____ you _____ tomorrow? (leave)
  B I'm _____ at 8 o'clock. (go)

b Complete the text with the correct form of the verbs in parentheses. Use contractions where necessary.

What color are our dreams?

[1] ___*Do*___ we ___*dream*___ (dream) in color or in black and white? People argued for many years about this question, and scientists [2] _____ (do) a lot of research about this question. One of these scientists is a psychologist who [3] _____ (work) at Dundee University. Her name is Eva Murzyn, and right now she [4] _____ (study) the effect of television on our dreams. Eva [5] _____ just _____ (publish) the results of her latest study.

Sixty people [6] _____ (help) Eva with her research. They completed a questionnaire and kept a diary of their dreams. She [7] _____ (choose) people who were either under 25 or over 55. When Eva analyzed their diaries, she [8] _____ (discover) that the younger people usually dreamed in color, whereas the older group often [9] _____ (have) black-and-white dreams. Eva thinks that this is because the older group [10] _____ (see) TV shows in black and white when they were young. She believes that something happened to their brains while they [11] _____ (watch) TV at that time.

2 VOCABULARY adjectives
+ prepositions

Circle the correct preposition.

1 Sleeping eight hours a night is good **for** / **to** you.
2 She's angry **with** / **at** him because he forgot her birthday.
3 Los Angeles is famous **to** / **for** its sunny weather.
4 I'm very bad **in** / **at** drawing.
5 Be nice **to** / **at** me today because I'm in a bad mood.
6 We aren't interested **about** / **in** auto racing.
7 My little sister is afraid **of** / **to** big dogs.
8 The new boss is very different **of** / **from** our old one.

3 PRONUNCIATION the letters *ow*

a **iChecker** Listen and circle the word with a different sound.

		aυ **ow**l	oυ ph**o**ne	
1	brown	know	how	town
2	blow	snow	now	show
3	borrow	crowded	shower	towel
4	low	throw	window	down

b **iChecker** Listen and check. Then listen again and repeat the words.

4 LISTENING

a **iChecker** Listen to a radio program about recurring dreams. Number the dreams in the order you hear them.

___ You are flying.
_1_ You are running.
___ You can't escape.
___ You are lost.
___ You are falling.

b **iChecker** Listen again and match the interpretations with the dreams.

Dream 1 | *e* | a You don't know what to do with your life
Dream 2 | ☐ | b You can't change a difficult situation.
Dream 3 | ☐ | c Your life has improved in some way.
Dream 4 | ☐ | d You don't want your life to change.
Dream 5 | ☐ | e ~~You don't want to face a problem.~~

USEFUL WORDS AND PHRASES

Learn these words and phrases.

flowers /ˈflaʊərz/
owl /aʊl/
psychoanalyst /ˌsaɪkoʊˈænlɪst/
violin /vaɪəˈlɪn/
freezing /ˈfrizɪŋ/
be frightened of /bi ˈfraɪtnd əv/
dream about /ˈdrim əˈbaʊt/
be successful /bi səkˈsɛsfl/

iChecker **TESTS** FILE 6

> I love your daughter, Jack. I love her more than anything.
> But frankly, sir, I'm a little terrified of being your son-in-law.
> *Greg in the movie* Meet the Parents, *2000*

1 GRAMMAR uses of the infinitive

a Complete the sentences with the infinitive of a verb from the list.

not do   find   not finish   rent   see   not tell   ~~wash~~

1 John's very polite. He offered _to wash_ the dishes after the meal.
2 Thanks for coming. We hope _____ you again soon.
3 She wasn't enjoying the lasagna, so she decided _____ it.
4 My boyfriend is unemployed. He needs _____ a job.
5 I'll tell you what she said, but please promise _____ anybody.
6 I'm sorry I shouted at you. I'll try _____ it again.
7 They want to live together. They're planning _____ an apartment.

b Write sentences using the adjective and the correct form of the verb.

1 **nice / meet**
Hello! How _nice to meet_ you.
2 **difficult / talk**
Do you find it _____ to my mom?
3 **easy / buy**
It's _____ presents for my best friend.
4 **important / not say**
It's _____ the wrong thing.
5 **great / hear**
Thanks for calling. It was _____ from you.
6 **fun / be**
It's _____ with your family.
7 **kind / invite**
Her parents were very _____ him.

c Complete the sentences with a verb in the infinitive.

1 He gave them some candy _to say_ thank you.
2 They're taking classes _____ Chinese.
3 We called the restaurant _____ a table.
4 He told us a joke _____ us laugh.
5 I went to an ATM _____ some money.
6 Do you use your phone _____ photos?

d Complete the sentences with a question word from the list and the infinitive of the verb in parentheses.

~~how~~   how many   how much   what   when   where

1 She gave me her address, but I don't know _how to get_ there. (get)
2 My brother is always busy, so I don't know _____ him. (call)
3 My mom asked me to get some eggs, but she didn't say _____. (buy)
4 We'd like to travel around the world, but we don't know _____ first. (go)
5 She wants to go to college, but she doesn't know _____. (study)
6 Who's going to be here for lunch? I have pasta, but I need to know _____. (make)

2 VOCABULARY verbs + infinitive

Complete the text with a verb from the list in the past tense.

forget   try   not want   promise   pretend   learn
offer   plan   ~~start~~   need   not remember

Charlie wasn't happy at his job, so he [1] _started_ to apply for a new job. Soon, one company called him and [2] _____ to give him in an interview. Charlie [3] _____ to tell his boss, so he [4] _____ to be sick. He told his boss that he had a stomachache, and he [5] _____ to go to the doctor's. His boss [6] _____ to call him later to ask him how he was. Charlie was really hoping to get the job, so he was a little nervous. He [7] _____ to drive to the interview, but there was a lot of traffic. In the end, he took the subway and was very late, and he [8] _____ to turn his cell phone off. Unfortunately, it rang while he was in the interview, but Charlie didn't answer it. However when his boss called later, he [9] _____ to act sick. The next morning, his boss said, "I'd like to see you in my office." Charlie [10] _____ to apologize, but his boss was very angry, and Charlie almost lost his job. But he [11] _____ an important lesson: not to lie to his boss again.

3 PRONUNCIATION linking, weak form of *to*

a Practice saying the sentences.

1 We want to know.
2 They hoped to win.
3 He promised to call.
4 I don't know what to do.
5 She forgot to go.
6 It's important to remember.
7 I learned to swim.
8 He started to cry.

b iChecker Listen and repeat the sentences.

4 READING

a Read the article. Is the writer generally positive or negative about mothers-in-law?

The truth about mothers-in-law

Although it's men who tell jokes about them, mothers-in-law are usually less popular with their daughters-in-law than with their sons-in-law. A recent study of 49 married couples found that two thirds of wives interviewed said that their mothers-in-law caused them "unhappiness and stress," compared with 15 percent of the husbands.

There are a number of reasons for this. First of all, there is the question of experience. A mother-in-law has already raised a family of her own, so she feels that she has a lot of knowledge to pass on. In this situation, it is very difficult for her to keep quiet. However, when a daughter-in-law is a new mother, she usually wants to find her own way of doing things. She often interprets her mother-in-law's advice as criticism, which can cause a conflict.

Secondly, there is the case of the husband. Both women care for him, although each of them loves him in a different way. On the one hand, he is the mother-in-law's son, and she obviously wants the best for him. On the other hand, he is the wife's partner, and she wants him to support her. Both women can get very upset if they see the man taking sides, and this can cause an argument.

However, mothers-in-law actually have a lot to offer, despite their reputation for causing trouble. They are generally excellent babysitters, and they don't mind helping with the housework. As long as they have their own independent lives and help out only when needed, mothers-in-law can play a very useful role in any family. The important thing is that they should not get too involved in their sons' and daughters' relationships so that nobody feels bad.

b Read the article again and choose the best answer.

1 What did the study find out about mothers-in-law?
   a More men than women have problems with them.
   b More men than women tell jokes about them.
   ⓒ More women than men have problems with them.
2 What advice do mothers-in-law try to give their daughters-in-law?
   a How to take care of their husband.
   b How to bring up children.
   c How to do housework.
3 According to the article, which situation makes daughters-in-law angry?
   a When their husband agrees with his mother.
   b When their husband talks to his mother.
   c When their husband argues with his mother.
4 Which women make the best mothers-in-law?
   a Those who are really close to their son.
   b Those who don't have a life of their own.
   c Those who know when to offer help.

c <u>Underline</u> five words you don't know. Use your dictionary to look up their meaning and pronunciation.

5 LISTENING

a iChecker Listen to a conversation between two people about a ban on mother-in-law jokes. Do they agree in the end? _____

b iChecker Listen again and complete the sentences with D (Dave) or J (Jane).

1 *D* thinks the ban is ridiculous.
2 __ thinks that the jokes are offensive.
3 __ thinks that it's important to have a sense of humor.
4 __ makes a joke.
5 __ thinks that the jokes don't show respect for parents.
6 __ mentions a historical fact about mothers-in-law.
7 __ quotes a historical joke.
8 __ says that the jokes are sexist.

USEFUL WORDS AND PHRASES

Learn these words and phrases.

advice /əd'vaɪs/
tactic /'tæktɪk/
greet /griːt/
survive /sər'vaɪv/
honest /'ɑnəst/
absolutely delicious /æbsəlutli dɪ'lɪʃəs/
be punctual /bi 'pʌŋktʃuəl/
make conversation /meɪk kɑnvər'seɪʃn/
shake (somebody's) hand /ʃeɪk 'hænd/
(make) the right impression /ðə 'raɪt ɪm'prɛʃn/

Happiness is when what you think, what you say, and what you do are in harmony.

Mahatma Gandhi, Indian political leader

1 GRAMMAR uses of the gerund (verb + -ing)

a Complete the sentences with the -ing form of the verbs in parentheses.

1 I hate ___being___ (be) cold. I find it really depressing.

2 You spend too long _____ (play) video games.

3 We stopped _____ (study) French because we didn't like the classes.

4 He's celebrating because he's finished _____ (write) his book.

5 It started _____ (snow) during the night while we were asleep.

6 I'm bored. I feel like _____ (go) for a walk.

7 My parents have bought a house by a beach because they love _____ (swim).

8 I don't mind _____ (get) up early in the morning.

9 Kathy really enjoys _____ (listen) to her iPod.

10 The best thing about _____ (take) the bus is _____ (not drive) in busy traffic.

b Match the sentence beginnings and endings.

1 Do you ever dream of ___c___

2 Are you interested in ☐

3 Please don't leave without ☐

4 She isn't very good at ☐

5 We ended the evening by ☐

6 I'm really looking forward to ☐

a doing some part-time work?

b seeing you tonight.

c ~~stopping work and retiring?~~

d thanking everybody for coming.

e saying goodbye to me.

f parking her father's car.

c Complete the text with the -ing form of these verbs.

drink	drive	exercise	get up	go	imagine	leave
listen	read	~~send~~	stay	take	turn	~~write~~

What makes you feel good?
Here are some more texts from our readers.

1 [1] ___Writing___ and then [2] ___sending___ a funny email or text message to my friends. And of course, [3] _____ their faces when they read it.

2 I really like [4] _____ at night when there's no traffic, [5] _____ to my favorite music. I feel completely free.

3 [6] _____ in bed on Sunday morning and [7] _____ the newspaper. Then [8] _____ very late and [9] _____ my dog for a long walk.

4 I enjoy [10] _____ to the gym and really [11] _____ hard, and then [12] _____ a nice cold drink followed by a long, hot shower. There's nothing better.

5 [13] _____ off my computer at the end of the day and [14] _____ work! It's the best moment of the day. I love it!

d Complete the text with the correct form of the verbs in parentheses (-ing form or infinitive).

Reading the digital way

Many of us who love [1] _reading_ (read) are changing our habits. Today, a lot of us have decided [2] _____ (use) E-readers, and so we've stopped [3] _____ (buy) traditional books.

E-readers have a number of advantages. They are very easy [4] _____ (carry), so they are ideal for people who like [5] _____ (travel). If you're abroad, and you don't have anything [6] _____ (read), you don't need [7] _____ (look for) a bookstore that has books in your language – you can download it as a digital book. In addition to this, E-readers are very private, so you don't need [8] _____ (show) people what you are reading. Finally, when you finish [9] _____ (read) a book, you no longer have to find room for it on a bookshelf.

However, there are some disadvantages. Some people say their eyes hurt if they spend a long time [10] _____ (look) at the screen. Also, you have to be careful [11] _____ (not lose) your E-reader or you'll lose all your books. In addition, if a friend would like [12] _____ (borrow) a book you've read, you can't offer [13] _____ (lend) it to them. With an E-reader, you can only continue [14] _____ (read) as long as the battery lasts, so you have to remember [15] _____ (take) your charger with you and you can't forget [16] _____ (charge) the battery.

2 VOCABULARY verbs + gerund

Match the sentences 1–6 with a–f.

1 He hates doing the housework. | c |
2 He feels like going for a run. | |
3 He doesn't mind cooking all the meals. | |
4 He's stopped playing basketball. | |
5 He spends hours chatting online. | |
6 He loves being with his friends. | |

a He doesn't do it anymore.
b It's OK for him to do it.
c ~~He really doesn't like it.~~
d He does it a lot.
e He wants to do it now.
f He really likes it.

3 PRONUNCIATION the letter *i*

a Circle the word with a different sound.

fish	1	miss	(mind)	skin	with
bike	2	traffic	nice	kind	size
fish	3	habit	finish	imagine	surprise
bike	4	right	give	invite	time

b **iChecker** Listen and check. Then listen again and repeat the words.

4 LISTENING

a **iChecker** Listen to five speakers talking about when and where they sing. How many of the speakers don't enjoy singing?

b **iChecker** Listen again and match the speakers with sentences A–E.

Speaker 1   _C_
Speaker 2   __
Speaker 3   __
Speaker 4   __
Speaker 5   __

A He / She does a lot of singing at work.
B He / She doesn't mind singing badly in front of other people.
C ~~He / She enjoys singing at home.~~
D He / She likes singing when he/she is traveling.
E He / She was in a choir at school.

USEFUL WORDS AND PHRASES

Learn these words and phrases.

soup /sup/
leftovers /ˈlɛftoʊvərz/
a feel-good movie /ə ˈfilgʊd ˈmuvi/
as soon as /əz ˈsun əz/
scales /skeɪlz/
breathe /brið/
choir /ˈkwaɪər/
high notes /haɪ noʊts/
magical /ˈmædʒɪkl/
bargain /ˈbɑrgən/

7C Learn a language in a month!

1 GRAMMAR *have to, don't have to, must, must not, can't*

a Look at the pictures. Complete the sentences with the correct form of *have to*.

1 A __*Do*__ teachers in your country __*have to*__ look stylish?
  B Not very stylish. They _____ wear formal clothes, but they _____ look neat.

2 A _____ American taxi drivers _____ work long hours? Someone told me that.
  B Yes. We _____ twelve hours a day, but we _____ work every day.

3 A _____ I _____ cook meals?
  B No. You _____ do the cooking, but you _____ help the children to eat.

4 A _____ your husband _____ travel abroad for his job?
  B No, he _____ travel abroad, but he _____ speak foreign languages.

b What do these signs mean? Write sentences with *must* or *can't*.

1 __*You must*__ pay in cash.
2 _____ turn left here.
3 _____ make a noise.
4 _____ use your cell phone.
5 _____ stop here.
6 _____ play soccer here.

c Complete the sentences with *must not* or *don't have to*.

1 The museum is free. You __*don't have to*__ pay.
2 You have to wear formal clothes. You _____ wear jeans.
3 The speed limit is 55 mph. You _____ drive faster.
4 Your hours will be 9–5 Monday to Friday. You _____ work on weekends.
5 That river is dangerous. You _____ swim in it.
6 It's a very small house. You _____ clean it every day.

2 VOCABULARY modifiers: *a little, really,* etc.

Order the words to make sentences.

1 ~~translation~~ / ~~useful~~ / ~~Online~~ / ~~aren't~~ / sites / very
  __*Online translation sites aren't very useful*__.
2 to / fairly / movies / understand / ~~It's~~ / American / difficult
  It's _____.
3 new / fast / speaks / ~~Our~~ / very / teacher
  Our _____.
4 of / little / those / unfriendly / a / students / ~~Some~~ / are
  Some _____.
5 is / English / idea / books / a / really / ~~Reading~~ / good
  Reading _____.
6 hard / extremely / Chinese / to / ~~It's~~ / learn
  It's _____.

3 PRONUNCIATION sentence stress

iChecker Listen and repeat. <u>C</u>opy the <u>rhy</u>thm.

1 You **must not** take **photos** here.
2 They **have** to take the **train** to **work**.
3 You **can't walk** on the **grass**.
4 We **don't have** to **go** to **school to**<u>day</u>.
5 You **must** take **one** pill <u>**every day**</u>.

4 READING

a Read the opinions about learning languages. Which do you think are the three best ideas?

What's the best way to...?
Learn a language
This week we ask students from all over the world for their ideas.

Gloria, Brazil

My favorite way to learn a language is to go to a language school and take a class. There are classes for many levels of English, whether you're beginning or you've been learning for a long time. It's great when you have other students in the class and you can learn and practice together, and of course, having a teacher to help you is really important. It's good to do your homework, too!

Ji-ho, South Korea

I think it's really hard to learn a language if you don't have anyone to talk to. I've joined a social networking site where I can chat in English to a lot of other people like me. I'm more interested in using English to communicate than anything else, so I don't mind if my grammar isn't perfect.

Paolo, Portugal

I don't have time to go to an English class, but there's a great site on the Internet that has classes in the form of podcasts. Every week, I download a few of these onto my phone so that I can listen to the class when I'm going to and from work. I find the words and phrases that I have to listen to and repeat extremely useful.

Suzen, Turkey

I'm a big fan of American pop music, so I spend a lot of time listening to different songs at home on my iPad. I've downloaded a new app that puts the lyrics on the screen and translates the song for you at the same time. I really enjoy learning English like this, and it's very good for my pronunciation, too.

Kiko, Japan

I can't afford to pay for one-on-one English classes, but I've found a great class online. I have to watch a short video, and then learn the grammar and vocabulary in it. If I have any questions, I can contact my online tutor who's very friendly. I'm really enjoying the class, and I've learned a lot from it.

Luis, Spain

I love books, and in my opinion, you can learn a lot of new words by reading in English. I look up difficult words with my dictionary or do a quick search online. Also, I can read a book whenever I want. I don't have to go to classes or pay a lot of money for private tutors. Books are great. I can learn English and about other subjects, too!

b Complete the sentences with the people's names.

1 _Suzen_ thinks that listening to songs helps her pronunciation.
2 _____ says that reading can improve your vocabulary.
3 _____ has contact with an online teacher.
4 _____ thinks that speaking is more important than grammar.
5 _____ likes meeting and practicing with other students.
6 _____ practices English mostly by listening.

5 LISTENING

a **iChecker** Listen to a radio program about the Cherokee language. On what gadgets can the Cherokee people use their language today?

_____

b **iChecker** Listen again and answer the questions.

1 How many languages exist in the world today? _About 6,000_
2 By 2100, how many will disappear?
3 How many members of the Cherokee tribe could speak Cherokee when the plan started?
4 How many Cherokees were there?
5 When did Apple release iOS 4.1 with Cherokee as an official language?

USEFUL WORDS AND PHRASES

Learn these words and phrases.

experiment /ɪkˈspɛrəmənt/
fees /fiz/
voice mail /ˈvɔɪs meɪl/
permitted /pərˈmɪtɪd/
obligatory /əˈblɪgətɔri/
complete beginner /kəmˈplit bɪˈgɪnər/
entrance fee /ˈɛntrəns ˈfi/
intensive course /ɪnˈtɛnsɪv kɔrs/
against the rules /əˈgɛnst ðə rulz/

iChecker **TESTS** FILE 7

1 VOCABULARY feeling sick

Complete the sentences by unscrambling the letters in parenthesis.

1 Dan feels terrible. He thinks he has the __*flu*__ (ULF).
2 I need to buy some tissues. I have a _____ (LCDO).
3 That fish wasn't very good. Now I have a _____ _____ (ACHOCHMSTAE).
4 You feel very hot. I think you have a _____ (EMRETUPETRA).
5 Please turn that music down. I have a _____ (CHAEHEDA).
6 Kate smokes too much. She has a _____ (OGUHC).

2 GOING TO A PHARMACY

Complete the dialogue with these words.

allergic	better	every	have	~~help~~
much	often	symptoms	take	well

A Good afternoon. How can I [1] __*help*__ you?
B I'm not feeling very [2] _____.
A What are your [3] _____?
B I have a bad cough.
A Do you [4] _____ a temperature?
B No, I don't.
A Are you [5] _____ to any drugs?
B No, I don't think so.
A Take this cough medicine. It'll make you feel [6] _____.
B How much do I have to [7] _____?
A Four teaspoons [8] _____ six hours.
B Sorry? How [9] _____?
A Every six hours.
B OK, thanks. How [10] _____ is that?
A That's $8.50, please.

3 SOCIAL ENGLISH

Complete the sentences.

1 **A** That was a l_____ meal.
   B I'm gl_____ you enjoyed it.
2 **A** C_____ I have some more coffee, please?
   B There isn't any more. Anyway, drinking too much coffee isn't good f_____ you.
3 **A** I think I sh_____ go now.
   B Would you like me to take you home?
   A No, I'll walk. I'm s_____ I'll be fine.

4 READING

Match the signs 1–9 with their meaning A–I.

1 | E | Do not exceed the stated dose

2 | |

3 | | Keep out of reach of children

4 | |    5 | | Watch your step    6 | |

7 | | May cause side effects

8 | | Not to be taken by infants   9 | | Take twice a day with a meal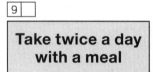

A You must keep this medicine where children can't find it.
B You must not give this medicine to small children.
C You must not drink this water.
D You must take this medicine at breakfast and dinner.
E ~~You should be careful not to take too much of this medicine.~~
F You should be careful if you feel sick after taking this medicine.
G You must not smoke here.
H You should be careful or you might fall.
I You have to turn your cell phone off.

Advice is what you ask for when you already
know the answer but wish you didn't.

Erica Jong, American writer

8A I don't know what to do!

1 GRAMMAR *should*

a Match the sentences with the pictures.
Complete them with *should* or *shouldn't*.

1 She ___should___ eat her vegetables. [B]
2 She _____ wear a coat. [ ]
3 "You _____ eat so much salt." [ ]
4 He _____ drive to work. [ ]
5 "You _____ get some glasses." [ ]
6 She _____ carry heavy bags. [ ]

b Complete the advice with *should | shouldn't* and
a verb from the box.

~~buy~~ call drink give go see tell

1 You _shouldn't buy_ it because it won't fit you.
2 You _____ coffee all day.
3 You _____ to bed earlier.
4 You _____ a doctor immediately.
5 You _____ her how you feel.
6 You _____ them any candy.
7 You _____ her and invite her to dinner.

c Read the problems A–G. Match them with the advice in **b**.

A I find it really difficult to get up in the morning, and
I'm often late for work. My boss has noticed, and she's
really angry with me. What should I do? [3]

B Yesterday, I hurt my foot while I was playing soccer.
It didn't seem very serious at the time, but now my foot
is black and blue. What is your advice? [ ]

C I've seen the perfect suit on sale in my favorite store,
and it's exactly what I'm looking for. The only problem
is it's a medium and I'm a large. What should I do? [ ]

D I really like one of my colleagues at work, and I think she
likes me, too. I'd really like to go out with her, but I don't
know how to ask her. Any advice? [ ]

E I have three children, and they all have terrible problems
with their teeth. We're always at the dentist's, and each
visit costs a lot of money. Any advice? [ ]

F I've always been very nervous, but now it's getting worse.
I don't have time to eat at work, so I drink five or six cups
of coffee during the day. What should I do? [ ]

G I've had an argument with my best friend, and I don't know
what to do. I feel very stupid, and I think I made a mistake.
What do you think I should do? [ ]

2 VOCABULARY *get*

Complete the sentences with the correct form of *get* and one of these words.

along	~~divorced~~	home	in shape	lost	
school	tickets	worse	up		text message

1 Her parents aren't happy together, so they're going to __*get*__ __*divorced*__.
2 Are your children in bed when your husband _____ _____ from work?
3 Our GPS wasn't working, and we _____ _____ on the way to our friends' house.
4 I'm going to the gym because I want to _____ _____.
5 The pain in my neck was _____ _____, so I went to the doctor.
6 This morning I _____ _____ for the concert online. They're very good ones in the front!
7 How well do you _____ _____ with your brothers and sisters?
8 I've just _____ a _____ from my boyfriend saying he's going to be late.
9 I don't feel like _____ _____ today. I'm going to stay in bed.
10 I often _____ to _____ late, although it's very close to where I live.

3 PRONUNCIATION /ʊ/ and /u/

a (Circle) the word in each group that has a different sound.

ʊ bull	1	pull	(food)	would
u boot	2	could	tune	soon
ʊ bull	3	took	pull	soup
u boot	4	book	do	two

b **iChecker** Listen and check. Then listen again and repeat the words.

4 LISTENING

a **iChecker** Listen to five speakers talk about a person they discuss their problems with. How many of them talk to members of their family?

b **iChecker** Listen again and match the speakers with the statements A–E.

Speaker 1   _C_
Speaker 2   __
Speaker 3   __
Speaker 4   __
Speaker 5   __

A has had some similar experiences to this person.
B also gives advice to this person.
C ~~is in a relationship with someone he/she met through this person.~~
D doesn't always agree with this person.
E first met this person when he/she was very young.

USEFUL WORDS AND PHRASES

Learn these words and phrases.

attend (a conference) /əˈtɛnd/
risk (verb) /rɪsk/
macho /ˈmɑtʃoʊ/
instead /ɪnˈstɛd/
avoid somebody /əˈvɔɪd ˈsʌmbɑdi/
be worth (doing) /bi wərθ/
change your mind /tʃeɪndʒ yər maɪnd/
go for (something) /goʊ fɔr/
keep in touch (with somebody) /kip ɪn tʌtʃ/

If everything seems to be going well, you have obviously overlooked something.

Murphy's Law

8B If something can go wrong...

1 GRAMMAR *if* + present, + *will* + base form (first conditional)

a Match the sentence halves.

Here are six more examples of Murphy's Law:

1 If you lose something, [c]
2 If you arrive early at a party, [ ]
3 If you make an appointment with the doctor, [ ]
4 If you don't do your homework, [ ]
5 If you buy a new rug, [ ]
6 If you get into a hot bath, [ ]

a you'll feel better before you see him.
b you'll drop something on it the first day.
c ~~you'll find it in the last place you look.~~
d the phone will ring.
e everyone else will be late.
f your teacher will ask you for it.

b (Circle) the correct form.

1 If the plane arrives late tonight, I (**will miss**) / **miss** the last bus.
2 If you **see** / **will see** an accident, call the police!
3 They won't get lost, if they **use** / **will use** their GPS.
4 We **don't get** / **won't get** to the movie theater in time if we don't leave now.
5 If you **don't take** / **won't take** an umbrella, it'll definitely rain!
6 If my phone **doesn't work** / **won't work** here, can I use yours?
7 Kathy **is** / **will be** disappointed if she doesn't get the job.
8 If there **isn't** / **won't be** much traffic when we leave, it won't take long to get there.

c Complete the texts with the correct form of the verb in parentheses. Then read and match the texts with the correct pictures, A–G.

Traditions and Beliefs

1 Giving a knife [D]
If a friend _gives_ (give) you a knife as a present and you _give_ (give) your friend a coin in return, your friendship _will last_ (last) forever.

2 Horseshoe [ ]
If you _____ (hang) a horseshoe above your door, it _____ (bring) good things to you and your family.

3 Ladders [ ]
If you _____ (walk) under a ladder, you _____ (have) bad things happen to you.

4 Throwing a coin in a fountain [ ]
If you _____ (throw) a coin into a well or fountain and _____ (make) a wish, the wish _____ (come) true.

5 Falling leaves [ ]
If it _____ (be) the first day of fall, and you _____ (catch) a falling leaf, you _____ (not be) sick all winter.

6 Mirrors [ ]
If you _____ (break) a mirror, you _____ (have) seven years of bad luck.

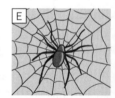

7 Spiders [ ]
If you _____ (see) a spider on its web, watch it carefully. If the spider _____ (run) down the web, you _____ (go) on a trip soon.

2 VOCABULARY confusing verbs

Complete the sentences with the correct verbs in the correct tense.

1 **look, look like**

You _look_ very stylish in that suit. In fact, you _look like_ a businessman!

2 **lose, miss**

I _____ my ticket, so I _____ the train and I was late for work.

3 **say, tell**

My son doesn't often _____ lies, but if he does, he always _____ sorry.

4 **hope, wait**

I'm _____ for the bus. I _____ it'll come soon because it's raining.

5 **look at, watch**

Our friends enjoyed _____ the video of our wedding, but they didn't want to _____ the photos of our honeymoon.

6 **know, meet**

She's _____ him since the summer. She _____ him on a business trip.

7 **borrow, lend**

If you need to _____ some money, I can _____ you 50 dollars.

8 **find, look for**

We were _____ a cheap apartment on the Internet, and we _____ the perfect place.

9 **carry, wear**

He was _____ a big coat and _____ a heavy suitcase.

10 **bring, take**

I'll _____ you to the airport if you _____ me back a souvenir.

3 PRONUNCIATION linking

a **iChecker** Listen to how the words are linked in each sentence.

1 If I walk, I'll arrive late.
2 It'll be hot if you go in August.
3 If it rains, I'll get a taxi.
4 She'll get angry if we don't invite her.
5 If we get up early, we can go to the mall.
6 If I don't understand the menu, I'll ask the waiter.

b **iChecker** Listen again. Practice saying the sentences.

4 LISTENING

a **iChecker** Listen to a radio program about natural disasters. How many tips does the expert give? _____

b **iChecker** Listen again and answer the questions.

1 Can you avoid natural disasters? _No, you can't._
2 During which months should you not go to the Caribbean? _____
3 What will travel insurance probably pay for? _____
4 Why is it important not to panic? _____
5 Who should you contact as soon as possible? _____
6 What should you ask your airline when you book your flight? _____

USEFUL WORDS AND PHRASES

Learn these words and phrases.

blizzard /ˈblɪzərd/
cyclone /ˈsaɪkloʊn/
earthquake /ˈərθkweɪk/
flood /flʌd/
forest fire /ˈfɔrəst ˈfaɪər/
monsoon /manˈsun/
tsunami /tsuˈnɑmi/
spill (coffee) /spɪl/
parking space /ˈparkɪŋ speɪs/
natural disaster /ˈnætʃrəl dɪˈzæstər/

8C You must be mine

1 GRAMMAR possessive pronouns

a Complete the questions and answers in the chart.

Whose...?	Possessive adjective	Possessive pronoun
1 *Whose bag is that* ?	It's my bag.	It's *mine* .
2 *Whose books are those* ?	They're your books.	They're _____ .
3 _____ ?	It's his laptop.	It's _____ .
4 _____ ?	They're her keys.	They're _____ .
5 _____ ?	It's our car.	It's _____ .
6 _____ ?	They're your coats.	They're _____ .
7 _____ ?	It's their house.	It's _____ .

b Complete the sentences with a possessive adjective (*my, your,* etc.) or pronoun (*mine, yours,* etc.).

1 **A** Are those __*my*__ glasses?
  B No, they're __*his*__ . __*Yours*__ are in your pocket!

2 **A** Whose coats are these? Are they _____ ?
  B Yes, they're _____ . Thanks a lot.

3 **A** Is that your husband's car? It looks like _____ .
  B No, it isn't. _____ car is bigger than that.

4 **A** Whose cat is that? It isn't _____ .
  B I've seen it in the neighbors' yard. I think it's _____ .

5 **A** Is that a new phone? _____ old one was black.
  B No, it's my sister's. _____ is broken, so I'm borrowing _____ .

2 VOCABULARY
adverbs of manner

Make adverbs from the adjectives in the box and complete the sentences.

calm dream lazy quiet serious ~~slow~~

1 Please walk more __*slowly*__ . You're going too fast!
2 Sorry? I can't hear you. You're speaking very _____ .
3 Mary hardly ever laughs. She takes things really _____ .
4 "I don't feel like doing anything today," he said _____ .
5 "I'd love to retire early and live on a tropical island," Mark said _____ .
6 Although all the passengers were worried, the flight attendant spoke _____ and explained the problem.

3 PRONUNCIATION
word stress

a Underline the stressed syllable.

1 de|tec|tive
2 dis|tance
3 do|llar
4 ad|van|tage
5 en|joy
6 com|plete|ly
7 re|mem|ber
8 pro|mise
9 su|spi|cious

b **iChecker** Listen and check. Then listen again and repeat the words.

4 READING

a Read the article about five famous chefs. Do you recognize any of them?

Ferran Adriá is a Spanish chef who is famous for preparing food scientifically. After serving in the military, Adriá got a job at elBulli in Catalonia, Spain as a line cook. He became head chef only 18 months later. elBulli closed in 2012, but it had three Michelin stars and was once voted the best restaurant in the world. Adriá has published several books and has taught a class at Harvard University.

Georges Auguste Escoffier was France's most important chef in the early 1900s. He was responsible for making traditional French food more modern and simple. He also made cooking food a respected job by introducing organized systems to restaurant kitchens. The French call Escoffier "the king of chefs and the chef of kings." He wrote cookbooks, cooked for royalty, and managed several restaurant kitchens during his successful career.

Jamie Oliver is one of the UK's best-loved TV chefs. His shows have been broadcast internationally in countries like the US, South Africa, Australia, Brazil, Japan, and Iceland. His books have been translated into thirty languages. Jamie is most famous for his campaigns to encourage schoolchildren to eat healthily. He's married with four children.

Tom Colicchio is a popular American chef and owner of Craft, a restaurant in New York City. He has always been interested in food and cooking, but he never graduated from a cooking school. He taught himself how to cook using French cooking guides. Despite this, he is the head judge on the reality TV cooking show *Top Chef* and the winner of five James Beard Foundation Medals for accomplishments in cooking.

Masaharu Morimoto is one of Japan's top chefs, and is well known for combining Japanese and Western food into delicious meals. He started his career as a baseball player at 17, but changed to cooking and opened his first restaurant at 24. Morimoto is probably most famous for starring in the TV reality shows *Iron Chef* and *Iron Chef America*, where he competes against other chefs in timed cooking battles.

b Read the article again and answer the questions. Write F, A, J, T, or M.

Who?
1 learned to cook by reading books   *T*
2 had a completely different job before becoming a chef   __
3 made cooking food easier   __
4 uses chemistry in his cooking   __
5 thinks young people should eat healthier   __

c Underline five words you don't know. Use your dictionary to look up their meaning and pronunciation.

5 LISTENING

a **iChecker** Listen to a conversation about an experiment on a TV show. Which question did the experiment hope to answer? Was it successful?

_____

b **iChecker** Listen again. Mark the sentences T (true) or F (false).

1 The show was on in the evening.   *T*
2 There were three cooks.   __
3 The rules for each course were that they had to use the same main ingredient and make the same dish.   __
4 There were two judges.   __
5 The cooks were professional restaurant critics.   __
6 Hugo only remembers two dishes because the judges found it very difficult to decide who made them.   __

USEFUL WORDS AND PHRASES

Learn these words and phrases.

advantage /əd'væntɪdʒ/
expenses /ɪk'spɛnsəs/
exclaim /ɪk'skleɪm/
trust /trʌst/
suspicious /sə'spɪʃəs/
calmly /'kɑmli/
dreamily /'driməli/
masterfully /'mæstərfəli/
the suburbs /ðə 'sʌbərbz/
somebody else /'sʌmbɑdi ɛls/

iChecker **TESTS** **FILE 8**

55

All animals are equal, but some animals
are more equal than others.
From Animal Farm by George Orwell, British writer

9A What would you do?

1 GRAMMAR *if* + past, *would* + base form (second conditional)

a Match the sentence beginnings and endings.

1 If my sister were older,   ☐ *f*   a if he could swim.
2 My parents would buy a bigger house ☐ b you'd be really scared.
3 He'd go sailing   ☐ c if they couldn't watch TV?
4 What would people do   ☐ d if it wasn't raining.
5 If you saw that horror movie,   ☐ e if they had more money.
6 I'd go for a walk   ☐ f ~~she could go to the party with me.~~

b Order the words to complete the sentences and questions.

1 car / would/ I / it / to / work / drive / a / had
   If I __*had a car, I would drive it to work*__ .
2 you / found / do / a / you / million / would / if / dollars
   What _____?
3 if / he / could / a / afford / one / phone
   He'd buy _____.
4 caviar / it / I / gave / me / wouldn't
   If someone _____.
5 say / could / talk / if / to / you / the / would / president / you
   What _____?
6 job / for / you / a / I / new / if / look / were
   I'd _____.

c Complete the second conditional sentences with the correct form of the verbs in parentheses.

1 If a bee __*flew*__ (fly) into my bedroom, I __*would open*__ (open) the window.
2 If my sister _____ (see) a mouse in the kitchen, she _____ (scream).
3 We _____ (not have) a dog if we _____ (not have) a yard.
4 If my brother _____ (not be) allergic to animals, he _____ (get) a cat.
5 If I _____ (live) in the country, I _____ (learn) to ride a horse.
6 What _____ you _____ (do) if a dangerous dog _____ (attack) you?

2 VOCABULARY animals

Complete the crossword.

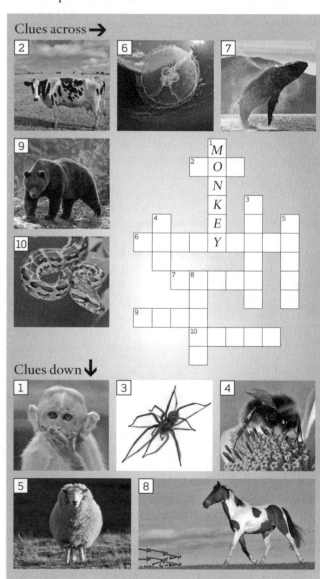

Clues across ➜

Clues down ⬇

3 PRONUNCIATION word stress

a Underline the stressed syllables.

1 bu|tter|fly	5 dol|phin	9 li|on	13 spi|der
2 ca|mel	6 e|le|phant	10 mon|key	14 ti|ger
3 chi|cken	7 gi|raffe	11 mo|squi|to	
4 cro|co|dile	8 je|lly|fish	12 ra|bbit	

b [iChecker] Listen and check. Then listen again and repeat the words.

4 READING

a Read the first part of the text and check (✓) the things you would do.

CROCODILE ATTACK!

If you were swimming at the edge of the water in Southern Florida in the US, and you saw a crocodile coming toward you, what would you do?

"I'd run away fast." ☐   "I'd pretend to be dead." ☐

"I'd try to open its mouth." ☐   "I'd put my fingers into its eyes." ☐

"I'd make a loud noise." ☐   "I'd try to fight it." ☐

b Now read the rest of the article. Circle the sentence that is the best summary.

1 There's nothing you can do if a crocodile attacks you.
2 There are a lot of things you can do if a crocodile attacks you.
3 There's only one thing to do if a crocodile attacks you.

Well, most of these are possible – the best thing to do depends on where the crocodile is at the time. If it comes toward you on land, experts say you should turn around and run away as fast as possible. Crocodiles can run faster than humans over a short distance, but they soon get tired. If they miss their first chance to catch their victim, they usually start looking for something else.

If you're in the water, then splash around to make a noise so that the animal gets confused. If this doesn't work, push your thumb or fingers into the crocodile's eye. This is the most sensitive area of the crocodile's body, and it is the place where you can cause the animal the most pain . It will also be very surprised by your attack, and it's possible that it will decide to leave you alone. Don't try and open the crocodile's mouth because the muscles are so strong that this is almost impossible.

However, if the crocodile is in a bad mood , it's possible that it will continue fighting. Your final opportunity is to pretend to be dead. If the crocodile thinks that its victim is dead, it opens its mouth for a few seconds to move the body into its throat. This can give you your last chance to escape, but it's a very dangerous plan.

Our final advice? It's much better to avoid crocodiles than to do any of the things above...

c Look at the highlighted words or phrases. Check their meaning and pronunciation with your dictionary.

5 LISTENING

a [iChecker] Listen to a news story about a shark attack. How did the man survive?

_____

b [iChecker] Listen again and answer the questions.

1 Where is Eric Nerhus from?

_____

2 What was he doing when the shark attacked?

_____

3 Which parts of his body were in the shark's mouth?

_____

4 What was Eric's vest made of?

_____

5 Who rescued Eric?

_____

6 How did Eric get to a hospital?

_____

7 What injuries did he have?

_____

8 How big was the shark?

_____

USEFUL WORDS AND PHRASES

Learn these words and phrases.

pockets /ˈpɑkəts/
backward /ˈbækwərd/
bite /baɪt/
float /floʊt/
shout /ʃaʊt/
sting /stɪŋ/
suck /sʌk/
tie /taɪ/
wave /weɪv/
keep still /kip ˈstɪl/

> I am not afraid of death, I just don't want to be there when it happens.
> *Woody Allen, American movie director*

1 VOCABULARY phobias and words related to fear

a Complete the phobias with the missing vowels. Then match them with the definitions.

1 *a g o r a* ph *o* b *i a*   [b]   a fear of spiders
2 cl__str__ph_b____   [ ]   b fear of open spaces
3 __r__chn__ph_b____   [ ]   c fear of heights
4 gl__ss__ph_b____   [ ]   d fear of closed spaces
5 __cr__ph_b____   [ ]   e fear of public speaking

b Complete the sentences with a suitable word.

1 Are you fr*ightened* of snakes? A lot of people are.
2 I'm very sc_____ of spiders. I don't like them much.
3 If you suffer from a f_____ of flying, you can't travel by plane.
4 My sister is te_____ of big dogs. She always crosses the street if she sees one.
5 My children don't like swimming. They're a_____ of water.
6 Elena has a ph_____ of insects. She never goes to the country.

2 GRAMMAR present perfect + *for* and *since*

a Circle the correct word to complete each sentence.

1 Jess hasn't flown on a plane **for** / **since** many years.
2 I haven't seen my parents **for** / **since** my birthday.
3 He hasn't ridden a horse **for** / **since** he fell off one when he was twelve.
4 We've had our rabbit **for** / **since** six months.
5 My grandmother has agoraphobia. She hasn't left the house **for** / **since** two years.
6 I've been afraid of dogs **for** / **since** I was very young.
7 Tomo is sick. He hasn't eaten **for** / **since** two days.
8 We haven't been back there **for** / **since** the accident happened.

b Complete the text with *for* and *since*.

A celebrity's life
Kristen Stewart, actress

Kristen Stewart has been a famous actress [1] *for* about five years now. She has been an actress [2] _____ she was eight years old, when her agent saw her performing at school. Her first role was in a movie where she didn't speak, but [3] _____ then she has been in many movies. She is probably best known for playing Bella Swan in *The Twilight Saga*, a part which she has played [4] _____ four years.

Kristen has lived in Los Angeles [5] _____ she was born. Because she was acting at a young age, she couldn't go to school, so she studied online. [6] _____ then, she has completed high school. She is now one of the best-paid actresses in Hollywood.

Something many people don't know about Kristen is that she has equinophobia, or a fear of horses. She has had this problem [7] _____ most of her life, but her fans have only known about it [8] _____ 2012, when she was making a movie with horses. Kristen explained that she has been scared of them [9] _____ she was nine years old, when she fell off a horse during a riding accident.

c Complete the questions about Kristen Stewart.
Use *How long* or *When* and the verb in parentheses.

1 <u>When did</u> Kristen Stewart <u>start</u> acting? (start)
 When she was eight.
2 _____ she _____ the part of Bella Swan?
 (play)
 For four years.
3 _____ Kristen _____ in Los Angeles? (live)
 Since she was born.
4 _____ Kristen _____ equinophobia? (have)
 For most of her life.
5 _____ fans _____ about her phobia? (hear)
 In 2012.

d Right (✓) or wrong (✗)? Correct the mistakes in the **bold** phrases.

1 **Nina hates flying** since she was a child.
 <u>Nina has hated flying</u> .
2 **How long time** has your brother been an actor?
 _____?
3 **We've been married** since 2000.
 _____.
4 He's been in the US **for February**.
 _____.
5 How long **do you have** your dog?
 _____?
6 He's had this job **since eight years**.
 _____.
7 I've had four cars **since I learned to drive**.
 _____.
8 **She's known Victoria** since they were at school.
 _____.

3 PRONUNCIATION sentence stress

iChecker Listen and repeat the sentences. Copy the rhythm.

1 **How long** have you **worked here**?
2 **How long** have they **been married**?
3 **How long** has she **known** him?
4 **We've lived** here for **six months**.
5 I've **studied English** for **three years**.
6 He's had a **phobia since** he was a **child**.

4 LISTENING

a iChecker Listen to a radio call-in program about phobias. What is cynophobia?

b iChecker Listen again and choose the correct answers.

1 The caller is worried about…
  a her pet.
  ⓑ someone in her family.
  c her phobia.
2 The dog bit…
  a the neighbor.
  b the caller.
  c the caller's son.
3 The caller wants some advice about…
  a preventing a phobia.
  b keeping dogs.
  c treating a phobia.
4 The psychologist tells the caller…
  a to keep her son away from dogs.
  b to talk about her son's experience with him.
  c to let her son play with a friend's dog.

USEFUL WORDS AND PHRASES

Learn these words and phrases.

cure /kyʊr/
drug /drʌg/
heights /haɪts/
overcome (a fear) /oʊvər'kʌm/
panic /'pænɪk/
afraid /ə'freɪd/
frightened /'fraɪtnd/
rational (opp *irrational*) /'ræʃənl/
scared /skɛrd/
terrified /'tɛrəfaɪd/
affect (somebody / something) (verb) /ə'fɛkt/
have an effect on (somebody / something) /hæv
 ən ɪ'fɛkt ɑn/

9C Born to sing

1 VOCABULARY biographies

a Complete the phrases.

1 My grandfather was [c]   a on his 65th birthday.
2 He went [ ]   b in love with my grandmother at school.
3 He fell [ ]   c ~~born in 1945~~.
4 He graduated from [ ]   d to school when he was five.
5 He started [ ]   e work when he was 19.
6 They got [ ]   f high school in 1963.
7 They had [ ]   g three children.
8 He retired [ ]   h married in 1968.

2 GRAMMAR present perfect or simple past? (2)

a Circle the correct verb forms.

My mother was born in Chicago, Illinois in 1948. When
¹(she graduated) / she's graduated from high school, she started
working in an office in Chicago. Later, the company ²sent / has
sent her to a different office in Denver, Colorado, where ³she
met / she's met my father. ⁴They fell / They've fallen in love,
and ⁵they got / they've gotten married in 1970. ⁶They had /
They've three children— I'm the youngest.

⁷They moved / They've moved back to Chicago again when my
father retired. They bought a very nice house, and ⁸they lived /
they've lived there for two years now. My father ⁹just planted /
has just planted a vegetable garden in the backyard— ¹⁰he was /
he's been an excellent gardener all his life. My parents
¹¹made / have made a lot of new friends, and they're very
happy in their new home.

b Write the verbs in the simple past or present perfect. Use
contractions where necessary.

1 **A** How long ___*have*___ you ___*studied*___ English? (study)
  B Since I was little. I ___*started*___ learning it at school.
  (start)

2 **A** Are Tom and Melissa married?
  B Yes, they are.
  A When _____ they _____ married? (get)
  B Last year. But they _____ together for about
  ten years now. (be)

3 **A** Is that man the new accountant?
  B Yes, he is.
  A How long _____ he _____ here? (work)
  B Only for two months. He _____ from college in
  June. (graduate)

4 **A** How long _____ you _____ your car?
  (have)
  B A long time! I _____ it in 2005, I think. (buy)

5 **A** When _____ Sandra _____ her
  best friend? (meet)
  B When she was at college. She _____ her for
  three years now. (know)

6 **A** How long _____ you _____ in Lima?
  (live)
  B Not long. I _____ six months ago. (arrive)

3 PRONUNCIATION word stress

a Write the words in the correct group.

~~award~~	~~children~~	college	divorced		graduate
married	musician	retire	separate (verb)		successful

1 Stress on 1st syllable	2 Stress on 2nd syllable
children	*award*

b 🔊 iChecker Listen and check. Then listen again and
repeat the words.

4 READING

a Read the text about John Lennon. Order the paragraphs 1–7.

John Lennon and his sons

A ☐ On December 8, 1980, one of John Lennon's fans shot him outside his apartment. Since then, both of his sons have become musicians. Julian Lennon has made six albums and Sean Lennon has sung and played bass guitar with a number of different bands. So far, however, neither of them have been as successful as their father.

B ☐ John Lennon was born in Liverpool on October 9, 1940. His parents separated when he was five, so he went to live with an aunt and uncle. However, he stayed in contact with his mother, who played him Elvis Presley records and taught him how to play the banjo.

C ☐ Before The Beatles broke up in 1970, John met the Japanese artist, Yoko Ono, and he divorced his first wife. He left the band and continued making music both on his own and with Yoko. Their son, Sean, was born on October 9, 1975 and John stayed at home to take care of him.

D ☐ When John was 15, his mother bought him his first guitar. He formed his first band called The Quarrymen while he was still at school. When he graduated from high school, he took classes at Liverpool College of Art but the band took up a lot of his time, so he didn't graduate from college.

E ☐ The band released its first single "Love Me Do" in October, 1962. They started touring the country. John married his first wife, Cynthia, in secret, and his first son, Julian, was born while they were away. Fans went crazy wherever The Beatles played, and all of their albums reached the number one spot on the charts.

F 1 The singer-songwriter and guitarist John Lennon is one of the greatest musicians of all time. Songs like "Give Peace a Chance" and "Imagine" made him famous all over the world.

G ☐ John met Paul McCartney at the second performance of The Quarrymen, and he soon joined the band. Later, George Harrison joined them as lead guitarist. In 1960, they became The Beatles, and they started looking for a drummer. Ringo Starr replaced their original drummer, Pete Best, in 1962.

b (Circle) the correct verb form in the questions.

1 When **was** / **has been** John Lennon born?
2 What **did his mother buy** / **has his mother bought** for him?
3 How long **were** / **have been** The Beatles together?
4 How long ago **did John Lennon die** / **has John Lennon died**?
5 How many albums **did Julian Lennon make** / **has Julian Lennon made**?
6 Which instrument **did Sean Lennon play** / **has Sean Lennon played** with different bands?

c <u>Underline</u> five words you don't know. Use your dictionary to check their meaning and pronunciation.

5 LISTENING

a [iChecker] Listen to a radio program about the American actress and singer Judy Garland and her daughter, Liza Minnelli. How old were they when they first performed on stage? _____

b [iChecker] Listen again and mark the sentences T (true) or F (false).

Both women…
1 were born in the US.   *T*
2 changed their names.   —
3 started performing when they were very young.   —
4 won Oscars.   —
5 sang together at the London Palladium.   —
6 had problems.   —
7 got married more than once.   —
8 had three children.   —

USEFUL WORDS AND PHRASES

Learn these words and phrases.

award /ə'wɔrd/
captain /'kæptən/
funeral /'fyunərəl/
injure /'ɪndʒər/
eldest /'ɛldəst/
respected /rɪ'spɛktəd/

talented /'tæləntəd/
be influenced by
 /bi 'ɪnfluənst baɪ/
(follow in somebody's)
 footsteps /'futstɛps/
form a band /fɔrm ə bænd/

Practical English Getting around

1 VOCABULARY directions

Complete the directions.

To get to the hotel you need to ¹turn left and go ²str_____ ahead until you get
to the roundabout. Go ³a_____ the roundabout and take the third ⁴e_____.
Then turn right at the traffic ⁵l_____ and ⁶t_____ the second turn on
the ⁷l_____. The hotel is called The Parker Hotel, and it's on the ⁸r_____.

2 ASKING HOW TO GET THERE

Complete the dialogue with the missing sentences.

How do I get to SoHo on the subway?   OK. Thanks. See you later.
OK. And then?   How many stops is that?
Could you say that again?   Where is it?

A ¹ _How do I get to SoHo on the subway?_
B Go to the subway station at Grand Central – 42nd Street. Take the
   6 train toward Brooklyn Bridge – City Hall. Get off at Spring Street.
A ² _____
B OK. Take the 6 train from Grand Central – 42nd Street to Spring
   Street.
A ³ _____
B Seven.
A ⁴ _____
B Then you can walk to the restaurant.
A ⁵ _____
B Come out of the subway on Spring Street. Go straight ahead for
   about 240 feet and the restaurant is on the right. It's called
   Balthazar.
A ⁶ _____
B And don't get lost.

3 SOCIAL ENGLISH

Complete the dialogue with the words in the box.

don't   feel   long   said   so   stay   think

A I'm ¹ _so_ sorry I'm late. I missed the bus.
B But you're always late.
A I ² _____ I'm sorry.
B Why don't you leave home earlier?
A Look, why ³ _____ we order? I'm really hungry.
B No. I don't want to ⁴ _____ here anymore.
A OK. Why don't we go for a walk? I can get a burger or something.
B I don't ⁵ _____ like a walk. It's been a
   ⁶ _____ day, and I'm tired.
A Listen. I'll take you home now. And tomorrow I'll make dinner for
   you at my house. What do you ⁷ _____?
B OK. I suppose that way you can't be late!

4 READING

Read the article and answer these questions.

1 How far is it from the airport
   to Manhattan?   _15 miles_
2 How long does it take to drive
   there when it isn't rush hour?   _____
3 How much does AirTrain JFK
   cost for two people one way?   _____
4 How much does a taxi cost for
   four people?   _____
5 How much do taxis charge
   per suitcase?   _____
6 What time is the earliest bus
   to Manhattan?   _____
7 How much is the fare for an
   adult and a six-year-old child?   _____

JFK International Airport

JFK (John F. Kennedy) International Airport is the largest
of the three airports serving New York City. It is located
in southeastern Queens, about 15 miles (24 km) from
Manhattan. Travel time to Manhattan by car during rush
hour can be over an hour; at other times it's about thirty
to forty minutes.

Getting into town from the airport

Although **AIRTRAIN JFK** does not travel directly to
Manhattan, it connects passengers to New York's subway
and bus networks. The trip costs $5 and takes about an
hour, depending on your destination. If you don't mind
carrying your own luggage, this is probably your best option.

TAXIS are available outside every terminal in the airport,
and there's a $52 flat fee plus tolls to any location in
Manhattan. Taxis will take up to four passengers, and there
is no additional charge for luggage.

NEW YORK AIRPORT SERVICE EXPRESS BUSES run every
20 to 30 minutes from 6:15 a.m. to 11:00 p.m. from each of
the airport terminals. The fare is $15 one-way, but you can
save money by buying round-trip tickets online. One free
child under 12 is included in the fare. You can choose to
get off at Grand Central, Port Authority, or Penn Station
and the ride takes about an hour.

b Underline five words or phrases you don't know.
   Use your dictionary to look up their meaning and
   pronunciation.

10A The mothers of invention

1 VOCABULARY verbs: *invent, discover*, etc.

Complete the sentences with the past participle of these verbs.

base	call	~~design~~	discover	give
invent	open	play	show	use

1 One World Trade Center in New York City was ___*designed*___ by the architect Daniel Libeskind.

2 The Statue of Liberty was _____ to the people of the US as a present from the French people.

3 Gold was _____ in California in 1848.

4 Lemons and sugar are _____ to make lemonade.

5 The game of rugby was first _____ at Rugby School in the UK.

6 The first public movie was _____ to an invited audience in Indiana in 1894.

7 The river that flows through Washington, D.C. in the US is _____ the Potomac.

8 The first game console was _____ by Ralph H. Baer.

9 Heathrow airport's Terminal 5 was _____ by the Queen in 2008.

10 Many characters in Somerset Maugham's books are _____ on real people.

2 GRAMMAR passive

a Order the words to make sentences.

1 discovered / were / Galileo / Saturn's rings / by /
   Saturn's rings were discovered by Galileo .

2 is / on / of / life / The movie *The Iron Lady* / the / based / Margaret Thatcher
   _____.

3 Apple / invented / Cell phones / by / weren't
   _____.

4 isn't / gas / Lead / in / used / nowadays
   _____.

5 sold / Low-cost flights / online / are
   _____.

6 an / were / architect / by / The Petronus Towers / designed / Argentinian
   _____.

7 wasn't / Steven Spielberg / *Avatar* / by / directed
   _____.

8 company / by / made / Minis / British / aren't / a / anymore
   _____.

b Write sentences in the present or past passive.

1 what / your new baby / named
   _What is your new baby named_____?

2 contact lenses / invent / a Czech chemist
   _____.

3 where / olives / grow
   _____?

4 the VW Beetle / design / in the 1930s
   _____.

5 diamonds / find / in many different colors
   _____.

6 when / vitamins / discover
   _____?

7 Spanish / speak / in Spain and many parts of
   South America
   _____.

8 where / the *Lord of the Rings* movies / make
   _____?

c Rewrite the sentences in the passive.

1 A factory in China makes these toys.
   These toys _are made by a factory in China_____.

2 People of all ages wear jeans.
   Jeans _____.

3 Microsoft didn't invent laptop computers.
   Laptop computers _____.

4 Does a computer control the heat?
   Is _____?

5 Stieg Larsson wrote *The Millennium Trilogy*.
   The Millennium Trilogy _____.

6 People don't use cassette recorders very much today.
   Cassette recorders _____.

7 Picasso didn't paint *The Scream*.
   The Scream _____.

8 Did the same person direct all the *Twilight* movies?
   Were all _____?

3 PRONUNCIATION –ed

a **iChecker** Listen and (circle) the past participle with a
different -ed sound.

1 dog	2 /ɪd/	3 dog	4 /ɪd/	5 tie
called discovered (painted)	checked invented pretended	opened wanted designed	rained started directed	decided produced based

b **iChecker** Listen again. Practice saying the words.

4 LISTENING

a Listen to a radio program about things
that have been invented by accident. Match the
inventions 1–3 with the inventors a–c.

1 The microwave oven [b]   a George Crum
2 The x-ray   [   ]   b Percy Spencer
3 Potato chips   [   ]   c Wilhelm Roentgen

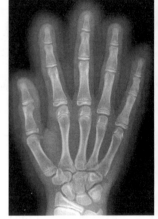

b **iChecker** Listen again and correct the sentences.

1 The discovery that microwaves heated food was
   made in ~~1954~~. *1945*

2 The microwaves melted a bar of chocolate on the table.

3 The man who discovered the x-ray machine was American.

4 He discovered that electrical rays could pass through
   water and air.

5 The image on the first x-ray is of the man's hand.

6 Thin fried potatoes are called potato chips by the British.

7 Their inventor was a waiter.

8 The potato chips were first called Saratoga potatoes.

USEFUL WORDS AND PHRASES

Learn these words and phrases.

hair dryer /'hɛr draɪər/
hammer /'hæmər/
knife /naɪf/
logo /'loʊgoʊ/
can opener /'kæn oʊpənər/
bullet-proof vest /'bʊlət pruf vɛst/
disposable diapers /dɪspoʊzəbl 'daɪpərz/
canned food /kænd fud/
windshield wipers /'wɪndʃild waɪpərz/

The beautiful thing about learning is that
no one can take it away from you.

B.B. King, American musician

10B Could do better

1 VOCABULARY school subjects

a Match the school subjects and the questions.

1 Foreign languages   `c`
2 Geography
3 History
4 Literature
5 Math
6 Physical Education
7 Science
8 Information Technology
9 Art

a What's 15 times 99?
b Who wrote *Macbeth*?
c ~~How do you say "thank you" in Portuguese?~~
d How do you select a program?
e When did Abraham Lincoln die?
f How many miles is eight laps around a standard track?
g Who painted *Three Musicians*?
h What's the capital of Argentina?
i What's the chemical symbol for water?

b Match the questions in **a** with the answers.

1 Buenos Aires   `h`
2 Pablo Picasso
3 *Obrigado*
4 1,485
5 William Shakespeare
6 H_2O
7 2 miles
8 Click on the icon.
9 1865

2 GRAMMAR used to

a Complete the sentences with the correct form of *used to* and the verb phrase.

1 [?] *Did you use to be* (you / be) a good student?
2 [−] I _____ (behave) very well.
3 [+] We _____ (wear) a uniform at school.
4 [?] _____ (Alex / have) a nickname to school?
5 [−] Students _____ (not study) IT when I went to school.
6 [+] Her school _____ (be) a same-sex school, but now it's coed.
7 [−] We _____ (not play) basketball in PE.
8 [?] _____ (your teachers / give) you a lot of homework?

b Correct the mistakes in the highlighted phrases.

1 I use to sit at the back of the class.   *I used to*
2 He used go to school on Saturday mornings. _____
3 We didn't used to understand our Spanish teacher. _____
4 Did you used to go to school by bus? _____
5 School use to start at 9:00 but now it starts at 8:30. _____
6 Did your friends use help you with your homework? _____

3 PRONUNCIATION used to / didn't use to

(iChecker) Listen and repeat the sentences. Copy the rhythm.

1 I **used** to be **good** at **math**.
2 **We used** to **hate** the **teacher**.
3 She **didn't use** to **like school**.
4 They **didn't use** to **wear** a **uniform**.
5 Did you **use** to play **soccer** in **PE**?
6 Did **your school** use to **open** in the **summer**?

4 READING

a Read the interview. Write the questions in the correct place.

Did you have a favorite teacher?

~~Where did you go to school?~~

Did you ever behave badly?

What's the most important lesson you learned at school?

What did you want to do when you left school?

What subjects were you good at?

My schooldays

DAVID SUCHET, actor, played Hercule Poirot in the TV series of Agatha Christie murder mysteries.
Interview by Tim Oglethorpe

1 *Where did you go to school?*
Grenham House, a boarding school in Kent, and Wellington School, a private school in Somerset.

2
One thing my schooldays did teach me was the importance of teamwork. At boarding school, I was an outsider and I was really, truly unhappy there. When I started playing sports at Grenham House, I became a member of a team, and I felt a lot better about myself. Like sports, acting is also almost always a team event, and you rely just as much on other people as they do on you.

3
Yes, I did. My brother and I both went to the same school and sometimes, we used to break the rules. In private schools at that time, a common punishment used to be "the cane": a long stick that the teacher used for hitting naughty boys.

4
Well, I wasn't very academic at all, really, and I was very bad at math. Luckily for me, I was really good at sports and that's the only reason they accepted me at Wellington. I was on the school rugby team, and I also played tennis. I played at Wimbledon once, in the junior tournament, and I got through to the second round.

5
Although I was good at sports, I never really considered taking it up professionally. Once I left Wellington, I wanted to become an actor, and I didn't play as many sports when I left school.

6
Yes, my favorite teacher was Mr. Storr, coach of the school tennis team, and also my English teacher. One day, when I was 14 or 15, I had to read in class. After the class, he said to me, "The way you read suggests you might enjoy acting. Would you consider playing Macbeth in the school play?" That was the beginning of my acting career, and I've never looked back since.

b Read the interview again. Mark the sentences T (true) or F (false).

1 He thinks it's important to work together with others. _T_
2 David didn't always enjoy his first school. ___
3 David wanted to be a tennis player when he left school. ___
4 He and his brother used to behave well. ___
5 In the past, a teacher could hit students with a stick. ___
6 David didn't use to be a very good student. ___
7 He only got into Wellington because he was good at sports. ___
8 Mr. Storr taught math and coached the tennis team. ___

c Look at the highlighted words. Use your dictionary to look up their meaning and pronunciation.

5 LISTENING

a **iChecker** Listen to two people talking about language learning in schools. Were Tony and Amy good at languages when they were at school?

_____

b **iChecker** Listen again and circle the correct answer.

1 Amy studied **Japanese** / **French** the longest.
2 Amy can remember one language more than the others because she **practiced it on vacation** / **studied it in college**.
3 Adults remember **some numbers** / **some adjectives** from their language classes.
4 According to Tony, some people are **too busy** / **too uncomfortable** to speak a foreign language.
5 **Spanish** / **Arabic** is more popular than French.
6 In the future, schools will **offer fewer languages** / **make younger students learn languages**.

The first step to getting what you want out
of life is this: Decide what you want.

Ben Stein, American writer

10C Mr. Indecisive

1 GRAMMAR *might* (possibility)

a Max and Sam are telling a colleague about their plans for next weekend. Complete the text with *might* and a verb from the box.

~~be~~ eat go have invite make rain take

"We feel like doing something special next weekend, but we haven't decided what to do yet. It [1] _might be_ sunny, so we [2] _____ for a walk by the river on Saturday. We [3] _____ lunch in a restaurant, or we [4] _____ some sandwiches with us.

On the other hand, it [5] _____, so we won't be able to go out. In that case, we [6] _____ some friends for dinner on Saturday. We [7] _____ dinner ourselves, or we [8] _____ out, we're not sure.
Everything depends on the weather, really."

b Complete the sentences with *might* or *might not* and a verb from the box.

be come fail get go ~~go out~~ have miss

1 I'm really tired so I _might not go out_ tonight.
2 Miguel doesn't speak English, so he _____ the job with the American company.
3 If you have a temperature, you _____ the flu.
4 My parents _____ to our party – they're thinking of taking a vacation then.
5 I haven't seen Johnny with Vanessa for a long time. They _____ together anymore.
6 If the taxi doesn't come soon, we _____ the train.
7 We love skiing, so we _____ to the Rocky Mountains for our next vacation.
8 Sue hasn't practiced much so she _____ her driving test.

2 VOCABULARY word building: noun formation

a Complete the chart with the correct noun or verb.

Verb	Noun
[1] *choose*	choice
confuse	[2] *confusion*
decide	[3]
[4]	death
educate	[5]
[6]	election
imagine	[7]
[8]	information
invite	[9]
[10]	life
opt	[11]
[12]	organization
[13]	success

b Complete the sentences with verbs or nouns from **a**.

1 After the _death_ of my grandfather, my grandmother came to live with us.
2 I made the right _____ to continue studying when I graduated from high school. I loved college.
3 They're going to _____ all their friends to their party.
4 _____ at school depends on how hard you work.
5 We're sorry to _____ passengers that the 4:30 train to Chicago is delayed.
6 He _____ to study history instead of geography at school.
7 Can you _____ a world without electricity?
8 The documentary was about the _____ of the author F. Scott Fitzgerald.

3 PRONUNCIATION diphthongs

a Check (✓) the pairs of words that have the same sound and put an (✗) for the pairs that don't.

1 m**igh**t	sc**ie**nce	✓
2 m**ay**	f**ai**l	__
3 kn**ow**	n**ow**	__
4 wh**ere**	w**ere**	__
5 h**ere**	th**ere**	__
6 t**ou**rist	**Eu**rope	__
7 sh**ow**	c**ow**	__
8 n**oi**sy	b**oy**	__

b **iChecker** Listen and check. Then listen again and repeat.

4 READING

a Read the text. What was the aim of the experiment? _____

_____

b Read the text again and circle the correct answer.

1 The participants in the experiment were all **in college** / **at work**.
2 The two groups were shown the card game **in different places** / **at different times**.
3 The participants had to go back **some time later** / **the next day**.
4 **Some** / **All** of the participants went to bed between the two visits.
5 There were **two** / **four** packs of cards in the card game.
6 The cards in the packs were **the same** / **different**.
7 The group who was taught in the morning **won** / **lost** more often than the other group.
8 The experiment helped researchers find a connection between **being creative** / **REM sleep** and making decisions.

c Highlight five words you don't know. Use your dictionary to look up their meaning and pronunciation.

Let me sleep on it

For many years, people have said that a good night's sleep often helps when you have to make an important decision. Research done recently by an American university has shown that this idea is actually true.

The researchers used a card game for their experiment, and 54 students between the ages of 18 and 23 took part. The scientists divided the participants into two groups. Both groups were given a short lesson on how to play the card game, either in the morning or in the evening. The lesson was very short—not long enough for either group to learn exactly how the card game worked. All of the students were asked to come back 12 hours later. The 28 students who had the class in the afternoon went home to a normal evening and their usual night of sleep, while the 26 who received the class in the morning came back after a day of normal activities without sleep.

On their second visit, the students played the game for long enough to learn that taking cards from the four different packs gave different results. Two of the packs had cards that helped players win more often while the other two packs had cards that made them lose. The object was to avoid losing the game.

In the experiment, the students who had had a normal night's sleep chose cards from the winning packs four times more than those who had spent the 12-hour break awake. The students who had slept also understood better how to play the game.

These results show that sleep helps a person make better decisions. The researchers think that this has something to do with rapid-eye-movement, or REM sleep, which is the creative period of our sleep cycle. The experiment shows that there is a connection between REM sleep and decision making, but researchers do not yet know what the connection is.

5 LISTENING

a **iChecker** Listen to five speakers talking about decisions they have made. How many of them made good decisions? _____

b **iChecker** Listen again and match the speakers with the sentences.

Speaker 1	C	A He / She thought time was more important than money.
Speaker 2	__	B He / She didn't get a special ticket.
Speaker 3	__	~~C He / She didn't arrive on time.~~
Speaker 4	__	D He / She didn't enjoy a special occasion.
Speaker 5	__	E He / She didn't accept an invitation.

USEFUL WORDS AND PHRASES

Learn these words and phrases.

products /ˈprɑdʌkts/
dissatisfied /dɪˈsætəsfaɪd/
indecisive /ˌɪndɪˈsaɪsɪv/
electrical gadgets /ɪˈlɛktrɪkl ˈgædʒəts/
be able to /bi ˈeɪbl tə/

make a decision /ˈmeɪk ə dɪˈsɪʒn/
miss an opportunity /ˈmɪs æn ɑpərˈtunəti/
pick somebody up (in a car) /ˈpɪk ˈsʌmbɑdi ʌp/
pick (something) /ˈpɪk/
take (something) seriously /teɪk ˈsɪriəsli/

11A Bad losers

1 VOCABULARY sports, expressing movement

a Complete the sentences.

1 The player took two shots to hit the golf ball into the h<u>ole</u>.
2 In track and field, the runners run in l_____ around a track.
3 It was m_____ p_____, and everyone was very tense, but his first s_____ went into the net.
4 The golf player had to try and hit the ball out of the b_____.
5 The athletes were running fast toward the finish line because they were on the last l_____.
6 When you take a p_____, you have to kick the ball past the goalkeeper.
7 The player who took the c_____ kicked the ball to a teammate, who headed it into the goal.

b <u>Underline</u> the prepositions of movement in **a**.

c Complete the crossword.

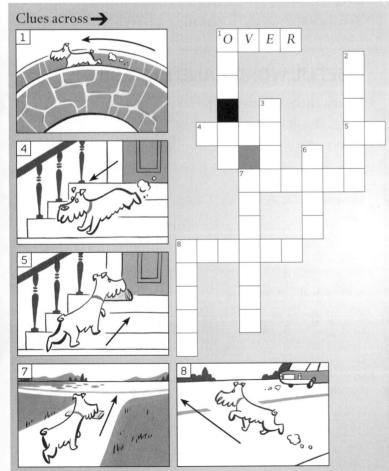

Clues across →

2 GRAMMAR expressing movement

a Look at the pictures. Complete the sentences with the simple past of the verbs and the correct preposition.

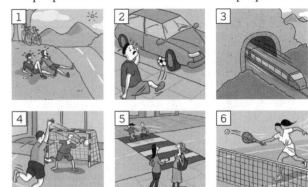

~~cycle~~ go hit kick run throw		
across into over through under ~~up~~		

In the ideal city...

1 They _cycled_ _up_ the hill.
2 The boy _____ the ball _____ the car.
3 The train _____ _____ the tunnel.
4 He _____ the ball _____ the goal.
5 The children _____ _____ the road.
6 She _____ the ball _____ the net.

Clues down ↓

b Look at the picture, read the story, and complete it with the prepositions.

across	into	out of	past	~~around~~
through	to	toward	under	along (x 2)

Last day at school for boy with dirty shoes!

Last Wednesday started as usual for 15-year-old Michael Brewster at Hove Park School.

At 10:30 a.m., Michael's class was jogging ¹ _around_ the gym. But when Charles Duff, the PE teacher, told Michael to clean his dirty sneakers, he got really angry. He ran ² _____ the gym, and back to the changing rooms where he found Mr. Duff's keys. From there, he went ³ _____ the parking lot, got ⁴ _____ Mr. Duff's Ford, and started the car. Then he drove ⁵ _____ the road, ⁶ _____ the bridge, ⁷ _____ the security guard, and ⁸ _____ the school gates. Then he turned left and drove ⁹ _____ the road for about 300 feet ¹⁰ _____ the math teacher's house. That was when he lost control. He tried to stop, but instead went ¹¹ _____ a field and crashed into a tree. Michael no longer attends Hove Park School.

3 PRONUNCIATION sports

a Look at the phonetics and write the sport.

1 /ˈsɑkər/   _soccer_
2 /ˈvɑlibɔl/   _____
3 /ˈɔtoʊ ˈreɪsɪŋ/   _____
4 /ˈskiɪŋ/   _____
5 /ˈwɪndsəfɪŋ/   _____
6 /ˈsaɪklɪŋ/   _____
7 /ˈbæskətbɔl/   _____
8 /ˈrʌgbi/   _____
9 /træk ænd fild/   _____

b **iChecker** Listen and check. Then listen again and repeat the words.

4 LISTENING

a **iChecker** Listen to five people talking about bad losers. Which games or sports do they mention?

_____

b **iChecker** Listen again. Who…?

1 lost a friend after playing sport with him / her _Speaker 2_
2 is on a team with someone who's a bad loser _____
3 has a parent who is a bad loser _____
4 used to let one of his/her children win _____
5 has a colleague who is a fanatical sports fan _____

USEFUL WORDS AND PHRASES

Learn these words and phrases.

coach /koʊtʃ/
corner /ˈkɔrnər/
hole /hoʊl/
lap /læp/
penalty /ˈpɛnlti/
beat /bit/
crash /kræʃ/
race /reɪs/
referee /rɛfəˈri/
score a goal /ˈskɔr ə goʊl/

11B Are you a morning person?

1 VOCABULARY phrasal verbs

a Complete what the people are saying in each picture.

1 Turn *down* the radio! It's very loud!
2 Don't worry! The game will be _____ soon.
3 We need someone who can look _____ our dog while we're on vacation.
4 Take _____ your shoes before you come in!
5 Can you fill _____ this form, please?
6 Put _____ a different jacket! That one looks awful!

b Complete the sentences with these verbs.

| find out | get along with | give up | go out | look forward to |
| look up | take back | throw away | try on | turn up |

1 Chris called the station to *find out* the times of the trains.
2 I never _____ empty jam jars. I wash them and then reuse them.
3 It's very cold in here. Can you _____ the heat?
4 The teacher told us to _____ the words we didn't understand.
5 We love traveling, so we always _____ our vacations.
6 I don't really like my sister's husband. I don't _____ him at all.
7 They only _____ on Friday or Saturday nights because they start work early during the week.
8 It's best to _____ clothes before you buy them.
9 We're going to _____ our new coffee machine because it doesn't work properly.
10 Anna's going to _____ candy and chocolate for a month to try to lose weight.

2 GRAMMAR word order of phrasal verbs

a Circle the correct phrases. If both are possible, check (✓) the sentence.

1 Please **turn off the lights** / **turn the lights off** before you go to bed. ✓
2 Thanks for the money. I'll **pay you back** / **pay back you** tomorrow.
3 I can't find my keys. Can you help me **look for them** / **look them for**?
4 Why don't you **try on that dress** / **try that dress on**? I think it'll suit you.
5 My mom usually **looks after my kids** / **looks my kids after** when we go out.
6 If you've finished playing, please **put the toys away** / **put away the toys**.

b Rewrite the sentences with a pronoun. Change the word order if necessary.

1 Can you write down **your email address**?
   Can you write it down ?
2 She'll give back **the exams** on Friday.
   _____ .
3 Are you looking forward to **your party**?
   _____ ?
4 I called back **my mother** when I got home.
   _____ .
5 We don't get along with **our new neighbors**.
   _____ .
6 Do you want to turn on **the TV**?
   _____ ?

3 PRONUNCIATION linking

iChecker Listen and repeat the sentences. Try to link the words.

1 Throw it away!
2 Turn it up!
3 Write it down!
4 Put it away!
5 Give it back!
6 Fill it out!

4 READING

a Read the article. Fill in the blanks with these phrasal verbs.

~~find out~~	get up	give up	go out
put on	take off	turn on	write down

b Read the article again. Check (✓) the people with good habits and put an (✗) next to the bad ones.

1 I go to bed every night at 11 o'clock.
2 I sleep for six hours during the week and ten hours on the weekend.
3 I always have lunch at my desk to save time.
4 I always wear sunglasses.
5 My bedroom is sometimes too cold.
6 I sometimes watch a movie to help me to go to sleep.
7 I usually have dinner at 7:30 p.m.
8 I often have a cup of coffee before I go to bed.
9 I keep a notebook by the side of my bed.
10 I sometimes meditate if I can't sleep.

c Look at the highlighted words or phrases and guess their meaning. Use your dictionary to look up their meaning and pronunciation.

5 LISTENING

a iChecker Listen to an interview with Jerry, a taxi driver who usually works at night. Is he positive or negative about his job?

b iChecker Listen again. Mark the sentences T (true) or F (false).

1 Jerry goes to sleep immediately after getting home from work. _F_
2 The first meal he has when he gets up is lunch. __
3 His children wake him up in the afternoon. __
4 He never feels tired when he wakes up. __
5 He eats three times a day. __
6 He doesn't mind his working hours. __

USEFUL WORDS AND PHRASES

Learn these words and phrases.

buzz /bʌz/
energetic /ɛnərˈdʒɛtɪk/
live (adjective) /laɪv/
sleepy /ˈslipi/
wild (night) /waɪld/
bowl (of cereal) /ˈboʊl/
any time /ˈɛni taɪm/
social life /ˈsoʊʃl laɪf/
set (your alarm clock) /sɛt/
stay in bed /ˈsteɪ ɪn bɛd/

Still tired in the morning?

Five tips for getting a better night's sleep

Sleep at the same times

[1] _Find out_ how much sleep you need and make sure that you get it. Go to bed and [2] _____ at the same time each day and you will have more energy than if you sleep the same number of hours at different times.

Make sure you are exposed to light during the day

Your body needs natural light to produce the hormone melatonin, which regulates your sleeping and waking cycle. Don't stay inside all day – [3] _____ during your lunch break , for example, for a short walk. On a sunny day, [4] _____ your sunglasses for at least half an hour to let light onto your face.

Create a relaxing routine before going to bed

Take a hot bath. Then [5] _____ your pajamas and make sure your bedroom is at the right temperature. Don't watch TV in bed because it will stimulate rather than relax you.

Avoid stimulants

Don't eat big meals or drink coffee late at night. Avoid drinking alcohol before you go to bed and [6] _____ smoking! Cigarettes can cause a number of sleep problems.

Getting back to sleep

If you wake up in the middle of the night and can't get back to sleep, try a relaxation technique like meditation. If that doesn't work, [7] _____ the light and read a book. If you're worried about something, [8] _____ your problem on a piece of paper so that you can deal with it in the morning.

If the tips above don't help, you might need to see a sleep doctor.

11C What a coincidence!

1 GRAMMAR so, neither + auxiliaries

a Complete the conversation with the phrases from the box.

~~Neither did I~~	Neither have I	Neither was I
So am I	So do I	So would I

A Hi, Tom. Do you ever watch *Who Do You Think You Are?* You know, that TV series about celebrities who find out about their families?

B Yes, I do. But I didn't see it last night.

A [1] _Neither did I_. I wasn't at home.

B [2] _____. But I usually watch it every week.

A [3] _____. I think it's really interesting. I'd love to find out about my family.

B [4] _____. I'm thinking about looking for some information on the Internet.

A [5] _____. But I haven't done anything about it yet.

B [6] _____.

b Respond to the statements with *So* or *Neither*, to say that you are the same.

1 I'm going out tonight.
   _So am I_____.

2 I enjoyed the party.
   _____.

3 I haven't done the homework.
   _____.

4 I was late today.
   _____.

5 I'm not hungry.
   _____.

6 I can't drive.
   _____.

7 I'd love to travel around the world.
   _____.

8 I don't have any pets.
   _____.

2 VOCABULARY similarities

Complete the text with words from the box.

as	both	identical	like
neither	~~similar~~	so	

People think my best friend Sue and I are sisters because we're very [1] _similar_. Sue's from the same town [2] _____ me, and we look a lot [3] _____ each other. We [4] _____ like shopping, and we have the same taste in clothes. I usually wear pants and tops, and [5] _____ does Sue. She doesn't like short skirts and [6] _____ do I. Once we went to a party together wearing [7] _____ clothes!

3 PRONUNCIATION sentence stress, word stress

a **iChecker** Listen to the sentences.

1 **So** did **I**.
2 **So** can **I**.
3 **So** have **I**.
4 **Neither** am **I**.
5 **Neither** do **I**.
6 **Neither** was **I**.

b **iChecker** Listen again and repeat the sentences. <u>Copy</u> the <u>rhy</u>thm.

c **iChecker** Listen and <u>underline</u> the stressed syllable. Then listen again and repeat the words.

1 i|den|ti|cal
2 si|mi|lar
3 co|in|ci|dence
4 a|maz|ing
5 dis|co|ver
6 ev|ery|where
7 per|so|na|li|ty
8 de|fi|nite|ly

73

4 READING

a Read the article and choose the best title.

1 A town with a mystery
2 The problems of having twins
3 Why couples have twins

Today, there are two thousand families living in the village of Kodinhi in southern India. Among them, there are more than 300 sets of twins, which is six times the global average. What makes this even more unusual is that India has one of the lowest birth rates of twins in the world.

Nobody can explain the reason why the village has so many twins. Some people say the cause might be genetic, but local doctor, Dr. Sribiju, doesn't think so. He says that there haven't always been twins in Kodinhi – parents suddenly started having them about sixty or seventy years ago. Neither does he believe that a new kind of pollution has caused the twins to be born. In that case, he argues, there would be more twins with birth defects. Luckily, most of Kodinhi's twins are born healthy. Dr. Sribiju thinks that the twins are born because of something the villagers eat and drink. He wants to discover just what that is, so that he can use it to help other couples who can't have children.

Having twins in this part of India can be a big problem for a family. It's expensive, and it can be dangerous for the mother's health. That's why the villagers of Kodinhi have started a support group . The group is called the Twins and Kin* Association, or TAKA for short. The president of the group is 50-year-old Pullani Bhaskaran, who has twin sons of his own. He wants all the twins in Kodinhi to join the group so that they can help each other. With the more than 300 pairs of twins in the village and the other people in their families, TAKA currently has 600 members.

Glossary
kin = family member

b Read the article and mark the sentences T (true) or F (false).

1 Parents don't usually have twins in India.   _T_
2 A century ago, there used to be more twins in Kodinhi.   __
3 Dr. Sribiju thinks that there are a lot of twins because of the pollution in Kodinhi.   __
4 Dr. Sribiju thinks that couples who want children could learn from the villagers of Kodinhi.   __
5 It can be a health risk for women in Kodinhi to have twins.   __
6 The president of TAKA has a twin brother.   __

c Look at the highlighted words and phrases and guess their meaning. Use your dictionary to look up their meaning and pronunciation.

5 LISTENING

a **iChecker** Listen to a radio program about famous twins. Match the twins (1–3) with the headings (a–c).

1 Romulus and Remus   _c_   a criminal twins
2 The Kray Brothers   __   b celebrity twins
3 The Olsen Twins   __   c historical twins

b **iChecker** Read the sentences. Listen again and write RR (Romulus and Remus), KB (the Kray Brothers), or OT (the Olsen Twins).

1 Their parents didn't want them.   _R R_
2 They were British.   ____
3 They're still alive.   ____
4 They met some very famous people.   ____
5 They had a serious argument.   ____
6 They became famous very young.   ____

USEFUL WORDS AND PHRASES

Learn these words and phrases.

tastes /teɪsts/	adopt (a child) /əˈdɑpt/
identical twins	by coincidence /baɪ koʊˈɪnsədəns/
/aɪdɛntɪkl ˈtwɪnz/	great to meet you /greɪt tə ˈmit yu/
security guard	go to college /goʊ tə ˈkɑlɪdʒ/
/sɪˈkyʊərəti gɑrd/	look exactly like /lʊk ɪɡˈzækli laɪk/

iChecker **TESTS** FILE 11

Practical English Time to go home

1 ON THE PHONE

Complete the dialogues.

1 **A** Hello, can I s_speak___ to Oliver, please?
   B T_his__ is Oliver.
   A Hi, Oliver. This is Mark. I'm r_eturning___ your call.

2 **A** Hi, Amy.
   B I'm s_____. You have the
   wr_____ number.

3 **A** Hello, this is reception. How can I help you?
   B Good morning. Mr. Clarke, please.
   A I'm sorry, the l_____ is b_____.
   B OK, can I l_____ a m_____?
   A Yes, of course.
   B Can you tell him Fiona called? I'll c_____
   b_____ later.

4 **A** Good morning, London 24seven.
   B Hello, can I speak to Alison, please?
   A Just a second, I'll p_____ you through.

2 SOCIAL ENGLISH

Circle the correct word or phrase.

1 **A** Does your boss know you're here?
   B No, I'll **call her** / **call to her** now.

2 **A** I've got a new job!
   B That's **great news** / **a great news**.

3 **A** I've got something to tell you.
   B Me, too. But you **do first** / **go first**.

4 **A** What are you doing here?
   B I'll explain **after** / **later**.

5 **A** Is everything alright?
   B **Never better** / **Ever better**.

3 READING

a Read the text. Which sentence is the best summary?

1 American and British English are almost exactly the same.
2 The most important difference between American and British English is the vocabulary.
3 Travelers don't have problems understanding American and British English.

American and British English

If you've learned American English and you're traveling in Britain, or if you've learned British English and you're traveling in the US, you'll notice some differences. An obvious difference is the accent, but most travelers find that they don't have too many problems with this. There are some grammatical differences, but they shouldn't make it difficult to understand people, or to communicate. That leaves differences in vocabulary, which can cause misunderstandings. Sometimes the difference is only the spelling, for example, in American English *center*, *color*, and *traveled*, and in British English *centre*, *colour*, and *travelled*. But sometimes the word is completely different in American and British English, so it's a good idea to be prepared.

b Match the American English with the British English.

1 check	c	a	taxi
2 fries		b	mobile
3 pharmacy		c	~~cheque~~
4 first floor		d	lift
5 elevator		e	ground floor
6 cell phone		f	chips
7 gas		g	queue
8 line		h	the underground
9 restroom		i	chemist's
10 store		j	toilet
11 cab		k	shop
12 sneakers		l	trainers
13 the subway		m	petrol

c Underline five words or phrases you don't know. Use your dictionary to look up their meaning and pronunciation. Make sure you can say them in American and British English.

12A Strange but true!

1 GRAMMAR past perfect

a Complete the sentences with the past perfect form of the verbs in parentheses.

1 The streets were white because it ___had snowed___ the night before. (snow)
2 I suddenly remembered that I _____ the windows before I left the house. (not close)
3 We got to the movie theater ten minutes after the movie _____. (start)
4 Tina felt nervous because she _____ before. (not fly)
5 Paul lent me the book after he _____ it. (read)
6 They missed the flight because they _____ the announcement. (not hear)

b Write questions in the past perfect.

1 **A** I drove my husband's car this morning.
  B you / drive it / before
  ___Had you driven it before___ ?

2 **A** My friends ate sushi in Japan.
  B they / eat sushi / before
  _____ ?

3 **A** My brother won a gold medal.
  B he / win a medal / before
  _____ ?

4 **A** The children made a cake yesterday.
  B they / make a cake / before
  _____ ?

5 **A** My sister ran the Boston marathon last weekend.
  B she / run a marathon / before
  _____ ?

6 **A** We went to Brazil on vacation.
  B you / be there / before
  _____ ?

c Make these two sentences into one. Use the past perfect and the simple past.

1 We bought some souvenirs. Then we went back to the hotel.
  After *we had bought some souvenirs, we went back to the hotel* .
2 Max did the ironing. Then he put the clothes away.
  After Max _____ .
3 They watched the news. Then they turned off the TV.
  After _____ .
4 I read the book. Then I gave it back.
  When _____ .
5 Ruth tried on the top. Then she went to the checkout.
  After Ruth _____ .
6 We had dinner. Then we did the dishes.
  After _____ .

d Circle the correct verb.

Last week my neighbor was on vacation. One night I [1] **heard** / **had heard** a strange noise in her house. I [2] **opened** / **had opened** the door to take a look, and I found that someone [3] **broke** / **had broken** into the house.

Luckily, he (or she!) [4] **already left** / **had already left** when I got there, and they [5] **didn't steal** / **hadn't stolen** much as far as I could see – just the TV.

I was looking for my cell phone yesterday morning, but I couldn't find it. I was sure I [6] **didn't lose** / **hadn't lost** it because I [7] **saw** / **had seen** it twenty minutes before. Then I realized that I [8] **left** / **had left** it in my pants pocket, and I [9] **put** / **had put** my pants in the washing machine!

2 PRONUNCIATION contractions: *had / hadn't*

a Write the sentences with contractions.

1 He had forgotten it.   *He'd forgotten it.*
2 We had lost it.   _____
3 You had seen her.   _____
4 It had been a terrible day.   _____
5 I had not sent it.   _____
6 She had not done it.   _____
7 They had not told me.   _____

b **iChecker** Now listen and check. Then listen and repeat the sentences. Copy the rhythm.

3 VOCABULARY verb phrases

Complete the sentences with the simple past or past participle of the verbs from the box.

get on	get out of	~~knock~~	realize	put
go on	take		leave	chase	belong

1 The professional boxer _knocked_ his opponent out.
2 The check-in clerk _____ my suitcase on the belt and gave me my boarding pass.
3 This ring _____ to my mother when she was young.
4 She wasn't worried because she had _____ the baby with her mother.
5 My parents weren't at home because they had _____ vacation a few days before.
6 After we had _____ the pool, we sunbathed for a while.
7 We went to the beach and _____ a swim.
8 When I got to my class, I _____ that I had forgotten my books.
9 After a thief stole my bag, I _____ him down the street and caught him.
10 The train left a few minutes after they had _____ it.

4 LISTENING

a **iChecker** Listen to four true news stories. Number the pictures in the order you hear the stories.

b **iChecker** Listen again and correct the mistakes in the sentences.

1 Someone took the Ranieri's ~~GPS~~. *cell phones*
2 The officer heard ringing from a bathroom.
3 Erin Langworthy was on vacation in Kenya.
4 She was taken to the hospital after she had walked to safety.
5 Lena Paahlsson lost the ring while she was doing the dishes.
6 Today the ring is too big for her.
7 The crocodile had gone into Jo Dodd's kitchen.
8 Mrs. Dodd called the Crocodile Management Center.

USEFUL WORDS AND PHRASES

Learn these words and phrases.

wave /weɪv/
arrest /əˈrɛst/
belong /bɪˈlɔŋ/
realize /ˈrɪəlaɪz/
steal /stil/

close to (adj) /ˈkloʊs tə/
outdoor /ˈaʊtdər/
fortunately /ˈfɔrtʃənətli/
net /ˈnɛt/
rob (a bank) /rɑb/

Gossip is what no one claims to like,
but everybody enjoys.
Joseph Conrad, Polish writer

12B Gossip is good for you

1 GRAMMAR reported speech

a Complete the reported speech.

Direct speech	Reported speech
1 "I want to leave him."	She said that she _wanted to leave him_____.
2 "I don't like her parents."	He told me that he _____.
3 "I'm getting divorced."	She told me that she _____.
4 "I've been to the police station."	He told me that he _____.
5 "I haven't met his girlfriend."	She said that she _____.
6 "I saw James with another woman."	He said that he _____.
7 "I can't cook."	She told me that she _____.
8 "I won't tell anyone."	He said that he _____.
9 "I'll speak to her tomorrow."	She said that she _____.
10 "I have a lot of work to do."	He told me that he _____.

b Write the sentences in direct speech.

1 She said she was busy.
   She said: "_I'm busy_."

2 Jane said that she wanted a cup of coffee.
   She said: "_____."

3 They told me that they hadn't seen the new
   neighbors yet.
   They said: "_____."

4 Steve told me that he didn't want to go to
   the movie theater.
   He said: "_____."

5 Helen and Paul said they would go to the party.
   They said: "_____."

6 He said that his computer had just broken.
   He said: "_____."

7 She told me that the city was very old.
   She said: "_____."

8 They said that they would visit me.
   They said: "_____."

2 VOCABULARY say or tell?

a Circle the correct words.

1 Her husband **said** / **told** that he was working late.
2 She **said** / **told** me that she wasn't happy.
3 They **said** / **told** us that they were getting married.
4 You **said** / **told** that she didn't like loud music.
5 I **said** / **told** you that I had a new laptop.
6 We **said** / **told** that we were going to be late.
7 Anna **said** / **told** you that she didn't have a car.
8 I **said** / **told** her that John was busy.
9 He **said** / **told** that we had to do exercise five.
10 You **said** / **told** that she had called Mike this morning.

b Complete the sentences with *said* or *told*.

1 She ___said___ that she had been to a friend's house.
2 We _____ our parents we wouldn't be home for lunch.
3 I _____ you that the man wasn't her brother.
4 They _____ that they were going on vacation.
5 He _____ me that he didn't have a cell phone.
6 You _____ that you weren't going out tonight.
7 James _____ that he was busy tonight.
8 I _____ that the movie started at eight o'clock.
9 We _____ them that his sister was on vacation.
10 Olivia _____ me that she had called Jack this morning.

3 PRONUNCIATION double consonants

a Look at the phonetics and write the words.

1 /ˈgɑsəp/   _gossip_
2 /ˈmærɪd/   _____
3 /ˈlɛtər/   _____
4 /ˈmɪdl/   _____
5 /ˈfʌni/   _____
6 /ˈdɪfrənt/   _____
7 /ˈdɑlər/   _____
8 /ˈsʌmər/   _____
9 /ˈmɛsɪdʒ/   _____
10 /ˈhæpi/   _____

b **iChecker** Listen and check. Then listen again. Practice saying the words.

4 LISTENING

a **iChecker** Listen to Alan and Jessica discussing a survey. Do they both gossip at work?

b **iChecker** Listen again and write T (true) or F (false).

1 _T_ Jessica and Alan think that women gossip more than men.
2 ___ According to the results of the survey, Jessica and Alan are right.
3 ___ The survey was done by a newspaper.
4 ___ Nobody was surprised by the results of the survey.
5 ___ Over 50 percent of the men in the survey said they gossiped at work.
6 ___ Less than 50 percent of women said they gossiped.
7 ___ The men in the survey talked about topics related to work.
8 ___ The women talked about their male colleagues.

USEFUL WORDS AND PHRASES

Learn these words and phrases.

genes /dʒinz/
gossip /ˈgɑsəp/
share /ʃɛr/
according to /əˈkɔrdɪŋ tə/
feel guilty /fil ˈgɪlti/
in general /ɪn ˈdʒɛnərəl/
pass on /ˈpæs ɑn/
social skill /ˈsoʊʃl skɪl/

79

How many roads must a man walk down
before you can call him a man?

Bob Dylan, US singer and songwriter

12C The *American English File* quiz

1 GRAMMAR questions without auxiliaries

a Circle the correct question.

1 a Who did paint *The Kiss*?
  b Who painted *The Kiss*?
2 a Which instrument does Yo-Yo Ma play?
  b Which instrument plays Yo-Yo Ma?
3 a How many lives do cats have in the US?
  b How many lives have cats in the US?
4 a What did happen in Japan on March 11, 2011?
  b What happened in Japan on March 11, 2011?
5 a Which American singer did die on June 25, 2009?
  b Which American singer died on June 25, 2009?
6 a Who did Beyoncé marry in 2008?
  b Who Beyoncé married in 2008?
7 a What animal caught a train for 31 miles?
  b What animal did catch a train for 31 miles?
8 a What invented Peter Durand in 1810?
  b What did Peter Durand invent in 1810?

b Match the questions in **a** with these answers.

a Nine.   3
b An earthquake and a tsunami.   __
c Michael Jackson.   __
d Gustav Klimt.   __
e Jay-Z.   __
f Canned food.   __
g The cello.   __
h A dog.   __

c Complete the questions for the answers.

1 What __made Mark Zuckerberg__ famous?
  Facebook made Mark Zuckerberg famous.
2 When _____ the soccer World Cup?
  Brazil won the soccer World Cup in 2002.
3 How long _____ together?
  REM stayed together for 31 years.
4 Who _____ Jack Sparrow in *Pirates of the Caribbean*?
  Johnny Depp plays Jack Sparrow in *Pirates of the Caribbean*.
5 How _____?
  Steve Jobs died from cancer.
6 Where _____?
  Polar bears live in the Arctic.
7 How many _____ at the Arc de Triomphe in Paris?
  Twelve roads join at the Arc de Triomphe in Paris.
8 Which country _____ in the world?
  India produces the most bananas in the world.

2 VOCABULARY review

a Circle the word or phrase that is different. Say why it's different.

1 curly   long   slim   straight
  It's not used to describe hair.
2 friendly   generous   kind   overweight
3 bracelet   earrings   necklace   warm-up suit
4 a crossword homework   a phone call housework
5 crowded   polluted   dangerous exciting
6 market   shopping   town hall department
              mall   store
7 decide   finish   forget   pretend
8 get up   get old   get in shape get lost
9 bee   butterfly bat   mosquito

b Complete the sentences with **one** word.

1 Why don't you try __on__ that dress?
2 She was born _____ March 24, 1996.
3 I'll have to take my new top _____ to the store. It has a hole.
4 Please don't throw _____ my old jeans. I still wear them.
5 You'll have to speak _____ the manager about your complaint.
6 I'm looking _____ to going away on the weekend.
7 The children ran _____ the road without looking. Luckily, there wasn't much traffic.
8 They arrived _____ Los Angeles at midnight.
9 We put the book _____ the desk in the library.
10 Can you please pick _____ that garbage from the floor?

c Complete the missing verbs.

1 g*o*_____ sightseeing
2 s_____ at a campsite
3 f_____ in love with somebody
4 m_____ a mistake
5 d_____ the dishes
6 l_____ money to somebody
7 s_____ hours doing something
8 g_____ along well with somebody
9 e_____ a salary
10 f_____ a job

3 PRONUNCIATION review

a Circle the word with a different sound.

æ cat	1	cap hat (want)
ʊ bull	2	book push school
u boot	3	lose hope suit
ʌ up	4	turn gloves sunny
eɪ train	5	lazy safe bald
oʊ phone	6	towel goat throw
aɪ bike	7	kind shy thin
aʊ owl	8	cow horse mouse
ɔr horse	9	boring four word
ɪr ear	10	beard earrings wear
ɛr chair	11	hair scared fear
k key	12	crowded city across
tʃ chess	13	church beach chemistry
dʒ jazz	14	large forget giraffe

b iChecker Listen and check.

4 READING

a Read the article and match the questions to the answers.

Don't ask me!

A survey of 2,000 parents has discovered that two thirds of them are unable to answer their children's questions about science. See if you can match the nine most common questions with their answers below.

1 Why is the moon sometimes out in the day? _D_
2 Why is the sky blue? ___
3 Will we ever discover aliens? ___
4 How much does the Earth weigh? ___
5 How do airplanes stay in the air? ___
6 Where do birds and bees go in winter? ___
7 What makes a rainbow? ___
8 Why are there different times on Earth? ___

A Bees stop flying and birds stay together in groups or migrate.
B People decided to have time zones so that it would be light during the day everywhere on Earth. If there weren't time zones, some people would have midday in the middle of the night!
C The Earth weighs around 13,200,000,000,000,000,000,000,000 pounds.
D The moon can be lit up by the sun, depending on where it is in the sky. If it reflects the sun's rays, we can see it, even during the day. It all depends on its angle toward the Earth.
E Sunlight arrives on Earth in every color, but it hits particles in our air that shine blue.
F Planes have special wings that push air down. This pushing action is stronger than gravity, and so the plane goes up in the air.
G Sunlight going through water drops in the air separates into all the colors.
H No one knows.

b Underline five words that you don't know. Use your dictionary to look up their meaning and pronunciation.

5 LISTENING

a iChecker Listening to five people talking about quiz shows. Complete the names of the shows.

1 _____ *My Line?*
2 *Cash* _____
3 *Wait Wait… Don't* _____ *Me!*
4 *Who Wants to Be a* _____ *?*
5 _____ *& Roll Jeopardy!*

b iChecker Listen again. Match some questions that could have been on these quiz shows with the speakers.

Speaker 1 _E_   A This US band wrote the song *Wake Me Up When September Ends.*

Speaker 2 ___   B Which US president is pictured on the $50-bill?
                    A Washington B Lincoln C Grant D Reagan

Speaker 3 ___   C Name seven countries that end in *–stan.*

Speaker 4 ___   D Which story is true?

Speaker 5 ___   E Do you use a computer for your job?

Listening

1 A))

Ben Great party.
Sandra Yes, it is.
Ben Sorry…hi…my name's Ben.
Sandra I'm Sandra.
Ben What do you do, Sandra?
Sandra I'm a nurse. How about you?
Ben Me? Oh, I'm a student.
Sandra A student? Really? What college do you go to?
Ben Columbia. I go to Columbia University. I'm in my second year of medical school.
Sandra Do you like it?
Ben Yes, I do. I like it a lot…

Ben What do you think of the music, Sandra? Do you like it?
Sandra No, not really.
Ben What kind of music do you listen to?
Sandra I like rock music.
Ben Do you? Who's your favorite band?
Sandra Muse. I really like Muse.
Ben Me, too. Did you go to the concert last month?
Sandra No, I didn't. Was it good?
Ben Yes, it was awesome. I'm sorry you missed it.

Ben Do you play any sports, Sandra?
Sandra Yes, I play tennis.
Ben Ah, nice. I play ice hockey. I'm on a club team.
Sandra Are you?
Ben Yes, I am. But I play tennis, too. Maybe we can play together one day.
Sandra Maybe. But I usually play with my boyfriend.
Ben Your boyfriend?
Sandra Yes, here he is. Wayne, this is Ben. Ben, Wayne.
Wayne Hello. Nice to meet you.
Ben Hi. Um, look at the time. Um, gotta go – some friends are waiting for me. Um, bye Sandra.
Sandra Bye.

1 B))

Host Hello, and welcome to *Love Online*. Today, we'd like you, the listeners, to call in and tell us about your experiences with online relationships. And – oh, my! – that's quick! – we already have our first caller. Hello?
Alan Hi, my name's Alan.
Host Hello, Alan. Can you tell us about your experience with Internet dating?
Alan Yes, of course. I'm pretty shy, you see, and I'm not very good at talking to girls I don't know. So one day, I registered on an online dating agency, and I met Susan.
Host And what happened?
Alan We got along really well. In fact, after four months, we got engaged.
Host Congratulations, Alan! Thanks for calling. Now, I think we have another caller. Hello?
Kate Hi, I'm Kate.
Host Hello, Kate. What can you tell us about love online?
Kate Well, I decided to try a dating site because I work long hours, and I don't have time to meet new people.
Host So what happened?
Kate Well, I met some guys, and then I met Craig.
Host Who's Craig?
Kate Well, now, he's my husband. We're very happy together and we're thinking of having children.
Host That's great news, Kate! It looks as if it is possible to find love online. Now, who's our next caller.
Paolo Paolo.
Host Hi, Paolo. Did you marry someone you met on the Internet?
Paolo Yes, I did, but it was the worst thing I ever did.
Host Oh. Why's that?

Paolo Because she didn't really love me.
Host How do you know that?
Paolo It was in the newspaper. There was an article about a woman who contacted men online, married them, and then left with all their money. And there was a photo of my wife next to the article.
Host Oh, I'm sorry to hear that, Paolo. And I'm afraid that's all we have time for today. Join me next week for another edition of *Love Online*…

1 C))

And now for the latest news in the art world. If you're in Paris this weekend, you might like to visit the new David Hockney exhibition called *Fresh Flowers*. As the name suggests, most of the pictures depict flowers. However, these are no ordinary flower pictures, because Hockney uses his iPhone or his iPad to draw them.

Hockney started painting on his iPhone during the winter of 2008. At the time, he was staying at his home in northern England where he has a beautiful view out of his bedroom window. One morning, he picked up his iPhone and used his fingers to paint the sunrise. He was very happy with the result, and started experimenting with other pictures. Now, he sends his friends a different flower picture every morning. They love it!

Fresh Flowers is at the Fondation Pierre Bergé, Yves Saint Laurent in Paris until January 30th. The exhibition shows the drawings Hockney made on an iPhone and the pictures he drew on an iPad. The gallery is open from 11 a.m. to 6 p.m. from Tuesday to Friday, and admission costs five euros. Don't miss this show; it will be a bright moment in your day.

2 A))

Speaker 1 When I was 17, I went on vacation with my parents to Brittany, in France. My parents rented a nice house on the beach, and the weather was great. We went for a delicious meal for my birthday, but I was miserable. I wanted to be with my friends, and I didn't smile once in two weeks!
Speaker 2 A few years ago, I went to visit an old school friend, but I didn't enjoy the weekend at all. At school we got along really well, but now she has two small children, so she didn't want to go out. I spent a very boring two days in her house watching TV. I don't think I'm going to visit her again.
Speaker 3 It's really hot where we live, so we always try to go on vacation where it's cool. Last year, we booked a vacation in Canada, but we arrived in the middle of a heat wave. It was awful because there was no air-conditioning anywhere. We just sat in cafes and argued all day. We can do that at home!
Speaker 4 When I finished college, I went on a cruise around the Mediterranean with some friends from my classes. We wanted to celebrate the end of our exams. As soon as we left the port, I started feeling seasick. I spent the whole week in bed, and I hated every minute of the cruise.
Speaker 5 Three years ago, I broke up with my boyfriend, so I decided to go on an expensive vacation on my own to the Seychelles. Unfortunately, the travel agent didn't tell me that the islands were popular with couples on their honeymoon. Everywhere I looked, there were people holding hands, and I felt very lonely.

2 B))

Jenny What should we do this afternoon, Matt?
Matt I know! Let's take a look at that box of photos my aunt gave me yesterday…Here it is…Oh, look at that!
Jenny Who's that?

Matt That's my grandfather. And that's my grandmother behind him on the right. She's the one in the flowery dress. It was just after they got married, before they had any children. My aunt told me all about this photo a few years ago.
Jenny So, where are they?
Matt Well, as you know my dad is Spanish. My grandparents lived in the center of Madrid, and this photo was taken in the district where they lived.
Jenny What's going on exactly?
Matt Well, there's a festival there called "La Paloma". It takes place in the middle of August every year, and it still happens now. There are lots of stalls selling food and also stalls where you can win a prize.
Jenny So, what was your grandfather trying to win?
Matt He was trying to win a bracelet for my grandmother. He was shooting at a target at the stall, and all those people were watching him.
Jenny Do you know any of the other people in the photo?
Matt No, I don't. But I think they all lived near my grandfather.
Jenny Who took the photo?
Matt The man at the stall. The photo was included in the price. You had three chances to hit the target, and you got the photo for free.
Jenny It's a great photo. I think your grandfather was very good-looking.
Matt That's what everyone says!

2 C))

Host Hello, and welcome to the program. Today, we're looking at lucky escapes, and Nick Williams from the news desk is here to tell us some amazing stories. Nick?
Nick Hi, Gloria. Well, my first story is about a tourist who fell into a volcano. Maureen Evason was walking at the top of the Teide volcano in Tenerife, when she tripped and fell. She fell 80 feet until she hit a tree, which stopped her fall and saved her life. The rescue operation took nearly four hours, and after that, Maureen spent two months in the hospital before she could go home.
Host Lucky Maureen! What else do you have for us?
Nick Joseph Rabadue had a lucky escape when he was at home watching TV. Joseph was sitting on the floor, so his father told him to go and sit on the sofa. Five minutes later, a truck crashed into their living room, and threw the family television into the air. The TV then landed on the exact spot where Joseph had been on the floor before.
Host What a lucky escape! Do you have anymore?
Nick Yes, just one more for now. One Saturday morning, Barry McRoy was leaving a cafe when two men came in. The men were fighting, and one of them had a gun. The man fired, and the bullet hit Barry in the chest. Luckily, he had a DVD in the pocket of his jacket at the time, and the DVD stopped the bullet. Barry McRoy is a very lucky man.
Host Absolutely! So, now it's time for you, the listeners, to call in and tell us about your own experiences. And here's our first caller.

3 A))

Dialogue 1
Woman 1 John!
Man 1 Hi, Jane. You look well.
Woman 1 You, too. How was your flight?
Man 1 We took off a little late, but it was fine.
Woman 1 Are you hungry?
Man 1 No, I had a sandwich on the plane.
Woman 1 Well, let's go and find the car. It isn't far.

Man 1 Great!

Dialogue 2

Check-in clerk Hello. Where are you flying to?

Passenger To Boston.

Check-in clerk Can I see your passport, please?

Passenger Here you are.

Check-in clerk Thanks. Can I see your carry-on luggage?

Passenger Yes, just this bag.

Check-in clerk OK. Here's your boarding pass. The flight is boarding at 4:50 p.m. from Gate B28. You're in Group B.

Passenger Thanks a lot.

Check-in clerk Enjoy your flight.

Dialogue 3

Immigration Officer Can I see your passport please, sir?

Passenger Here you are.

Immigration Officer What is the purpose of your visit, Mr. Green?

Passenger I'm going to stay with a friend.

Immigration Officer And how long are you going to stay in San Francisco?

Passenger For three weeks.

Immigration Officer Can I have a contact telephone number, please?

Passenger Yes. My friend's number is 415-555-7020.

Immigration Officer Thank you, Mr. Green. Enjoy your stay.

Dialogue 4

Woman 2 Look! There's a gray suitcase. Is it ours?

Man 2 No, it's too big. Ours is much smaller.

Woman 2 It's taking a long time to come out…

Man 2 Yes. The first one came out really quickly.

Woman 2 Look! There it is! Finally!

Man 2 You stay here with the other bags. I'm going to get it.

Woman 2 OK. I'll wait for you here.

Dialogue 5

Customs Officer Excuse me, ma'am. Can you come this way, please?

Passenger Yes, of course.

Customs Officer Do you have anything to declare?

Passenger No, I don't think so. I bought some chocolate in the duty-free store, but that's all.

Customs Officer Can I check your bag, please?

Passenger Sure. Go ahead.

Customs Officer OK…That's fine. You can go on through.

Passenger Thank you.

3 B)))

Chris Hi, Dawn. I hear you're going to be on vacation next week.

Dawn Yes, I am. And I'm really looking forward to it.

Chris What are you going to do?

Dawn I'm taking a train trip through Mexico with a friend.

Chris A train trip? I did that when I was a student. I traveled with very little money, not much food, and no sleep. It was fun, but I don't want to do it again.

Dawn Ah, but you see taking a train trip as an adult is very different.

Chris Really? In what way?

Dawn Well, to start with, I'm going to travel first class, so it'll be much more comfortable.

Chris How long are you going for?

Dawn I wanted to go for two weeks, but work's so busy right now… so just ten days.

Chris And which places are you visiting?

Dawn Chihuahua, Creel, Divisadero, Cerocahul, and Los Mochis. We're starting in El Paso, Texas, in the US and ending in Los Mochis in Mexico. We're driving to Mazatlan at the end of the trip because we want to spend a few days at the beach.

Chris What about sleeping arrangements? Are you going to sleep on the train?

Dawn No, there aren't any sleeping compartments on this particular train, so we're sleeping in hotels

every night. We're having most of our meals in the dining car of the train, though. I'm looking forward to enjoying my meals as the Mexican countryside goes by.

Chris Well, it sounds like a different kind of trip than the one I went on as a student.

Dawn Absolutely. It's going to be different, but I'm sure we're going to have a lot of fun.

3 C)))

Host Hello, and welcome to *The World of Words*. Today, we're going to look at word games, so let's start with the most popular of them all: *Scrabble*. Ricky Jones from the National Scrabble Association is here to tell us all about it. Ricky, who actually invented the game?

Ricky Well, it was an American named Alfred Mosher Butts. Butts was an unemployed architect, and in his free time he did a lot of crossword puzzles. These crossword puzzles gave him the idea for a game that he called *Lexico*. The game had the same letter tiles as *Scrabble*, but no board. Players used the letter tiles to make words. They scored by adding up the points on each of the letter tiles. Later, Butts introduced a board, and a set of rules and changed the name to *Criss-Cross Words*.

Host How did Butts decide how many points to give each letter?

Ricky He counted how many times each letter appeared on the front page of the *New York Times*. Then, depending on the frequency of each letter, he gave it between one and ten points. The most common letters, like the vowels, got only one point because they are easier to use. There are more of these letters in the game. There was only one tile for each of the least common letters, for example Q and Z, which got ten points.

Host So, when did Butts' original game become the modern game of *Scrabble*?

Ricky Well, in 1948, Butts met a businessman named James Brunot, who designed a new board and changed the name of the game to *Scrabble*. Then in 1952, the president of Macy's, the famous New York department store, discovered the game on vacation, and loved it so much he placed a large order. Butts and Brunot knew they couldn't produce enough *Scrabble* sets for Macy's, and so they sold the rights to the game to another manufacturer. Today, *Scrabble* is sold in 121 countries in 29 different languages.

Host What a story, Ricky! Thank you for sharing it with us.

Ricky My pleasure.

4 A)))

Speaker 1 Housework? Me? No, that's my mom's job. She only goes to work two days a week, so she has enough time to cook and clean and things like that. I go to school and then I see my friends, so I'm too busy to do housework. My dad goes to work every day, so he doesn't have time either.

Speaker 2 Well, I try and help my mom when I can. I make my bed when I get up in the morning, and I always set the table for dinner. I usually clean my room, but my mom is the one who cleans it. Apart from that, I'm not at home very much, so I don't do anything else.

Speaker 3 Oh, yes. Everyone in my family helps with the housework. There are four of us and we're all very busy. During the week, my mom or my dad cooks the dinner, and my brother and I do the dishes. We do the cleaning together on Saturday mornings.

Speaker 4 It's true – I don't do much housework, but I love cooking. I don't have time to cook during the week, but I do all the cooking on the weekend. My mom does all the cleaning, though. She says she doesn't mind it.

Speaker 5 We have a cleaning lady who comes in every day and she does all our housework. She makes the beds, cleans the floors, and cleans our rooms – she even does the ironing! I'm not sure who does the shopping, but the refrigerator is always full. That's the important thing!

4 B)))

Host Those listeners in the US who enjoy going shopping will be interested to hear our next news story. There are many wonderful shopping malls in the US, but did you know that a new mall in London is one of the most stylish places to shop these days? It's taken six years and 2.35 billion dollars to build, but the Westfield shopping mall has opened in Stratford, in East London. We sent our reporter, Juliet Redditch, over to take a look at what is now Europe's largest urban shopping mall. Juliet, what's it like in Westfield right now?

Juliet Well, Terry, there are crowds of people everywhere, especially outside the stores that have special opening sales. Some stores have called security staff to help them control the lines.

Host Just how big is Westfield, Juliet?

Juliet Oh, it's very big! There are two enormous department stores, a huge supermarket, and 300 smaller stores. You can spend all day here if you want to. I haven't decided where I'm going to have lunch, but there are 70 different places to eat – it's amazing!

Host What effect has the shopping mall had on the local area, Juliet?

Juliet Well, this is an area where there are many people out of work. The shopping mall has created 10,000 new jobs, so it has really helped.

Host How did you get to Westfield today?

Juliet I came by car. There's an enormous parking lot with space for 5,000 cars. But you can also get here by bus, train, and on the Tube – it's the best connected shopping mall in the country.

Host Now, Juliet, the big question is…have you bought anything yet?

Juliet No, I haven't. I was just looking around, really. I saw some pants I liked, but I didn't buy them. There were too many people in the fitting rooms to try them on!

Host OK, thanks Juliet, and now onto a news story of a different kind…

4 C)))

Speaker 1 Last weekend was really awful. My husband and I went camping in the mountains with some friends, and it rained the whole time. It was really depressing. We had to stay in the tent and play cards all day, which was OK to begin with, but then my husband got bored. He started complaining about the weather, and then about our friends, and finally about me! We had a terrible argument, and in the end we came home on Saturday night. I'm never going camping again!

Speaker 2 My weekend was great. I took my wife to Paris, which is somewhere she has wanted to visit her whole life. We stayed in a wonderful hotel, in a beautiful old building overlooking the river. The view was incredible. We ate some really great food, and although it was cold, we had a very nice walk around the city. The best part was that it was a surprise for my wife: I met her after work on Friday, and we drove straight to the airport. She had no idea where we were going!

Speaker 3 I don't have much money right now, so I didn't do anything special this weekend. But actually, I had a really good time! I visited a local museum with some friends. All the museums here are free, and they have some interesting exhibitions about places like Egypt, Rome, and India. We then watched two of my favorite DVDs on Saturday night, and on Sunday I invited my parents to my apartment, and I cooked dinner for them. Not a bad weekend, really.

Speaker 4 My brother and his wife stayed with us this weekend. They have three children, and we spent the whole time playing with them. We took them swimming, we went to the zoo, and on Sunday we went to the park. They have so much energy! And they're really noisy – especially in the morning when they wake up, which is usually around 6 o'clock. I was completely exhausted by Sunday night, but it was great to see them.

5 A 🔊

Speaker 1 Well, I haven't been here long, so I haven't had time to make many friends yet. After I get home from work, I spend most of the evening online chatting with friends and family back home. Twice a week, I take classes to try and learn the language. Most of my colleagues speak very good English, but I haven't been out with them yet.

Speaker 2 I guess you could say I'm a little depressed right now. Time goes really slowly when you don't have anything to do. I spend more time sleeping now, and I have a lot of time to do the housework. It doesn't take all day to make the bed and clean my room, so I get really bored. I hope I find another job soon because I really need the money.

Speaker 3 My life has changed a lot now that I don't have to leave the house to go to work. Things aren't so stressful first thing in the morning now. I just get up, make a cup of coffee, and turn on my computer. It's strange communicating with colleagues online and not seeing them face-to-face. Sometimes, it gets a little lonely.

Speaker 4 Oh, no, I never get bored. There's always so much to do! I like to get up early and read the newspaper while I'm having breakfast. Then I like to go for a walk and do some shopping. After lunch, I go and pick up my grandchildren from school. We spend an hour in the park until their mother comes to get them. I'm really enjoying life right now.

Speaker 5 This is the best thing that has ever happened to me! She's so beautiful that I seem to spend all day looking at her! I don't have time to see friends now, so I keep in touch with everybody by phone or online when she's asleep. We go shopping together, and I do more housework and cooking, but I don't get much sleep anymore!

5 B 🔊

Host Hello, and welcome to *The Travel Program*. Now, one of the most popular tourist destinations these days is the amazing country of Brazil. Sonia Medina from the Brazilian Tourist Board is here to tell us all about it. Sonia, what's so special about Brazil?

Sonia Oh, Brazil is a very large country, and there's just so much to see and do there. First of all, there are historic cities like Salvador – the first capital of Brazil – and Rio de Janeiro to visit.

Host Let's start with Salvador. What's there to see there?

Sonia Well, Salvador is in the eastern part of the country on the Atlantic Ocean. It's both an old city and a modern one at the same time. There are a lot of very tall office buildings and great shopping malls there, and the city has a lot of museums – one of the most important is the Museu de Arte da Bahia.

Host What about Rio de Janeiro?

Sonia Rio de Janeiro is a little bigger than Salvador – the population is about six million. It's in the southern part of Brazil, also on the Atlantic Ocean. Rio de Janeiro has churches dating back to the 16th century, famous cultural landmarks, and world-class sports. In my opinion, Rio de Janeiro is one of the most exciting cities in the world.

Host Apart from the cities, what else would you recommend?

Sonia The beaches. There are wonderful beaches northeast of Rio de Janeiro – especially on the peninsula of Búzios, which has more than 20 of them. You can drive or take a bus there from Rio de Janeiro.

Host Is there anything to do in Búzios besides going to the beach?

Sonia Well, if you are a fan of water sports, you can sail a boat, surf, or windsurf. There are also a number of restaurants to enjoy as well as interesting stores to explore.

Host So, when is the best time to visit Brazil, Sonia?

Sonia The main tourist areas are very crowded from December to March, so it's better to go between May and October, when it isn't as busy and hotel prices are a little lower.

Host Thank you, Sonia. Brazil certainly sounds like a very exciting vacation destination. Now, let's look at a different type of vacation…

5 C 🔊

Dave Hey, Alice. Let's take this quiz. It says you can find out your body age.

Alice Body age? OK.

Dave You first. So…we start with your real age, which is 35…

Alice Don't tell everyone.

Dave Sorry…then we add or subtract years depending on your answers to the questions. Got that?

Alice Yes.

Dave OK, then. First question. How much do you walk a day?

Alice Well, I always go for a walk at lunchtime. So…a lot.

Dave A lot. OK, so we subtract one year, which leaves us with 34. Next question. How many sports do you play and how often do you exercise?

Alice Oh, I hate playing sports. And I don't exercise at all. I guess that means none.

Dave No sports or exercise. Add two years. That makes 36. How much fast food do you eat?

Alice None. I don't eat any.

Dave Great! Subtract a year. We're back on 35 again. How many servings of fruits and vegetables do you eat?

Alice A lot. I have more than five every day.

Dave A lot. Subtract two years. That's 33. Next one. How would you describe yourself mentally?

Alice Um, what do you mean?

Dave Well, are you a positive person, or a negative person?

Alice Oh, right. Um, I think I'm a very positive person.

Dave OK. Subtract three years…Now you're at 30. Next question. How would you describe your stress level?

Alice Mmm, I would say I'm a little stressed…but it's under control.

Dave OK, so we don't have to add or subtract anything. You're still at 30. How many close friends do you see regularly?

Alice Mmm. A few. I don't have much time.

Dave OK…we don't add or subtract anything again. Last question. How much time do you have for yourself?

Alice Not enough. I'm always really busy.

Dave Add a year…That makes 31. Which means that you are 35, but your body is only 31. What do you think of that?

Alice 31? That's great news! Now it's your turn…

6 A 🔊

Matt What are you reading?

Amy Nothing. Just my horoscope.

Matt Really? What sign are you?

Amy Virgo. My birthday's on September 15th.

Matt So, what does it say?

Amy It says that people will talk about me next week because of something I've done.

Matt But you don't really believe that, do you?

Amy Well, actually I do…because I've done something that will make people talk about me.

Matt Oh. What have you done?

Amy I sent an email to my boss yesterday complaining about my new colleague. She's really lazy, and she never does any work.

Matt Did you?

Amy Yes. So my boss will ask the other people in my office about this new person and he'll probably ask about me, too. So, my horoscope is right. People will definitely talk about me next week.

Matt Well, don't worry about it. I'm sure everything will be alright.

Amy I hope so.

Matt Anyway, what about me? What does my horoscope say?

Amy Let me take a look. Your birthday's January 5th, so that makes you…a Capricorn.

Matt That's right….so, what does it say?

Amy It says…oh! Listen to this! It says you'll get some money next week.

Matt Really? Maybe I should go out and buy a lottery ticket!

Amy No, wait a minute. Let's think about this. You have a meeting with *your* boss tomorrow, don't you?

Matt Yes. Why?

Amy Maybe she'll give you a raise!

Matt Oh, Amy! Really! You're taking this far too seriously! I don't believe a word of it!

Amy Well, I do. I think your boss will raise your salary tomorrow. Maybe she'll offer you a better job!

Matt Amy, you're being a little too optimistic. It's only a horoscope!

6 B 🔊

Speaker 1 I was on vacation, and I was looking around a famous palace, when a man came up to me and asked me to take a photo of him. He gave me his camera, but it wasn't working properly. When I gave it back to him, he dropped it on the floor and it broke. I picked it up and went to give it to the man, but he was gone. Then I discovered my wallet was missing.

Speaker 2 When I went abroad last year for a business trip, I didn't have time to get any local money before I left. So after I landed, I went straight to the bank to get three hundred dollars. I was in a hurry because I had a train to catch. The cashier slowly counted out the bills and when he stopped, I picked them up. When I got to the train station I realized later that I only had a hundred dollars.

Speaker 3 When we were on vacation, two men knocked on the door of our apartment. They were wearing uniforms and they said they were police officers. One of them came in to look around while the other stayed by the door. Unfortunately, while we were talking to the first man, the second man took our wallets and cameras from the bedroom.

Speaker 4 I was having a problem using the ticket machine in the subway when someone came up to help me. He told me how much money I needed and then offered to put it in the machine for me. I counted out the money, but he said it wasn't enough. I gave him some more money and I got my ticket. Unfortunately, I paid ten times the price for it!

Speaker 5 I was waiting at a bus stop, when this beautiful woman came up to me. We started talking, and she invited me to go to a restaurant with her. We had dinner together, and then the waiter brought me an incredibly expensive check. I started to complain, but then I noticed four big men at the door who were looking at me. Of course I paid the check.

6 C 🔊

Host Hello, and welcome to the program. Do you ever have the same dream night after night? These dreams are called recurring dreams, and psychologist Dr. William Harris is in the studio today to tell us all about them. Good morning, Dr. Harris.

Dr. Harris Hello.

Host Dr. Harris, which is the most common recurring dream?

Dr. Harris Well, at the top of the list is the dream where someone or something is running after you. Either it's a person or a dangerous animal, like a bull or a lion. The dream means that there's something in your life that you don't want to face. It can be a feeling, a conflict, or a memory, for example, but whatever it is, it's something that you don't want to deal with.

Host OK. What's the next dream on the list?

Dr. Harris It's the one where you are falling for what seems like a very long time. Falling is a definite sign that you are out of control. You have lost direction in your life, and you don't know what to do.

Host Yes, I've had that dream before. Not recently, though. Anyway, what other recurring dreams are there?

Dr. Harris This is another fairly common dream. You're trying to get somewhere but you get lost on the way, and you don't know where you are. People often have this dream when they're going through a period of change. It shows that they don't want to accept the new situation.

Host OK, Dr. Harris. Do you have anymore recurring dreams for us?

Dr. Harris Yes, there are two. The first dream is a good one. Some people have a recurring dream that they are flying through the air. They are enjoying it, and enjoying looking down on the world below. This shows that they are feeling free, possibly because they have solved a problem they had, or they have escaped from a difficult situation in their life.

Host And the last dream?

Dr. Harris This one isn't so good. It's a feeling of being trapped. Maybe you are in an elevator that's trapped between floors and you can't get out. This dream means that there is something in your life that's making you feel unhappy, and you feel that you cannot change it.

Host Dr. Harris, that was very interesting. Thank you for talking to us.

Dr. Harris You're welcome.

7 A))

Dave Oh, that's ridiculous!

Jane What is?

Dave They've decided to ban jokes about mothers-in-law!

Jane Who has?

Dave The government. They've written a brochure for workers who have to deal with the public, and it says that mother-in-law jokes are "offensive."

Jane Well, I suppose they are, really. I mean, there are a lot of mothers-in-law out there, and the jokes are about them.

Dave No, but it's just fun, right? I mean, I think it's really important to have a sense of humor. It's good for you – it makes you feel better.

Jane That's easy for you to say, isn't it? You're a man, so you'll never be a mother-in-law. I will, one day.

Dave Yes, but you won't be my mother-in-law, will you? Sorry, I was only joking!

Jane Ha ha…Does it say anything else about the jokes?

Dave It says they show "disrespect for parents."

Jane OK. Well, maybe they do. Young people are healthy, fit, and attractive. It's easy for them to laugh at older people, don't you think?

Dave Oh, come on! These jokes about mothers-in-law have been around since Roman times.

Jane Where did you get that idea from?

Dave It says here that there's a Roman writer named – hang on a minute – named Juvenal who said in the first century A.D. – wait, listen to this – "it's impossible to be happy when one's mother-in-law is still alive." Ha ha! That's classic!

Jane Um.

Dave And all the best comedians tell jokes about mothers-in-law, too. I think they're funny.

Jane Like I said, that's because you're a man. And the comedians you're talking about are also men. It's just another example of the sexist world we live in. I mean, there aren't many jokes about fathers-in-law, are there?

Dave Oh, for goodness' sake!

7 B))

Speaker I like singing while I'm taking a shower. The bathroom is a great place to sing because nobody can hear you – at least, I hope nobody can hear, because I sing really loudly! I usually sing very old classic songs, which I'd never sing in public!

Speaker 2 I always feel like singing when I'm alone in my car on a summer's day. I turn up the radio, open the window, and sing along to whatever comes on. I don't do this in the middle of town, of course; only if I'm driving through the country, but I must say I find it really relaxing.

Speaker 3 I've always really enjoyed singing with the kids I teach – I'm an elementary school teacher. Young children love singing, and they like it even more if the songs have actions. It's amazing how much they learn

from songs – there are alphabet songs, counting songs, and all kinds really. We always have a lot of fun when we're singing together.

Speaker 4 Actually, I can't sing very well at all, so I'm always really embarrassed if I have to sing in public. When I was in high school, I had to be in the school choir, but I never actually sang. I just mouthed the words and pretended to sing.

Speaker 5 When I'm out with my friends, we sometimes go to a karaoke in town. It's one of my favorite places because we always have a good time. We spend most of the evening singing together and nobody seems to mind if we do it badly. In fact, it's better if we do sing badly because it makes everybody laugh.

7 C))

Host …And here's some good news for one of the world's endangered languages. There are about six thousand languages in the world today, and experts say that nearly half of them are dying out. That means that around three thousand languages will disappear in the next century or so. One language in danger of dying out is the Cherokee language, spoken by the Cherokee people of North America. Or at least it *was* in danger until the leaders of the tribe decided to do something about it. They got worried when they realized that only 8,000 of the 290,000 Cherokee people in the world today actually spoke the language and they came up with a plan. They got in touch with the electronics company, Apple, and asked them to include Cherokee on the official list of languages used on their products.

At first, it seemed impossible that Apple would take any notice of the Cherokee because their products already had fifty languages on them. The big surprise came in September 2006, when the Apple iOS 4.1 operating system was released with Cherokee on the official list of languages. Since then, the Cherokee people have been able to use their language on all Mac computers, iPhones, the iPod Touch, and the iPad. These devices were popular with the younger members of the tribe from the start, but now the older members are taking an interest, too – especially those who use cell phones. So, it looks as if the Cherokee language won't die out just yet after all. And if the language stays alive, the culture will stay alive, too, something that the leaders of the tribe will be very happy about.

8 A))

Speaker 1 I don't usually talk about my problems, but if something's going wrong, I sometimes mention it to Phil. He's on my basketball team, and we get along OK. In fact, he's the one who introduced me to the girl I'm dating right now.

Speaker 2 The person who I talk to most is my sister. We don't look like each other at all, but we both have very similar personalities. She's a really good listener, and she always gives me good advice. She sometimes tells me her problems, too, and I try to help her.

Speaker 3 My friend Jenny is in some of my classes at college, and I tell her absolutely everything. We're very different, which means we often think in different ways. Sometimes we argue, but we're never angry with each other for long – just until one of us apologizes.

Speaker 4 The person who understands me most is my friend John, who lives next door. We've grown up together, so he knows me pretty well. My main problem right now is my job, which I hate. John thinks I should look for a new one, and he's probably right.

Speaker 5 My grandma lives with us, and I spend a lot of time talking to her. Although she's older than me, she's always interested in what I have to say. We have a lot in common, and some things that have happened to me also happened to her when she was young.

8 B))

Host Now, everyone loves traveling, and we all enjoy telling stories about the places we've been to. But what happens if there's an earthquake while you're away? Travel expert, Monica Fields, is here in the studio with

us today to give us some tips on what to do in a natural disaster. First of all, Monica, is it possible to avoid them?

Monica Well, no, actually, it isn't. Nobody really knows exactly when a disaster like a forest fire or a blizzard will happen, so you can't really avoid it. What you can do, however, is be prepared.

Host How can you do that?

Monica Well, first of all, if you plan to visit a region where there are natural disasters at certain times of the year, try not to go at that time. For example, there are often bad storms, hurricanes, or cyclones in the Caribbean in August and September, so don't go there then.

Host That sounds sensible. What else can you do?

Monica It's really important to buy travel insurance before you go. This will pay for extra nights in a hotel, for example, if you can't fly home and have to stay at your resort longer than you had planned. I never understand why some people don't get travel insurance.

Host Right. So, what should you do if a natural disaster actually happens while you're abroad?

Monica The first thing you should do is to stay calm and be patient.

Host That sounds easy, Monica, but natural disasters can be very frightening, can't they?

Monica Yes, of course, but if you panic, things will only get worse. Secondly, you need to contact your family and friends at home as soon as possible. If they hear about the disaster on the news, they'll be extremely worried.

Host Yes, I can see that. What else should you do?

Monica Well, it's always a good idea to know what your airline will do if there's a natural disaster. If you are flying to a country where natural disasters are frequent, you should ask your airline when you book your ticket if they will change your ticket if you need to leave the country quickly, or if you have to stay longer because there is a natural disaster.

Host Thank you for joining us, Monica, and thanks for your useful advice.

8 C))

Hugo Did you watch TV last night, Kim?

Kim No, I didn't. What was on?

Hugo There was a really interesting cooking show on after dinner.

Kim There was? What made it so good?

Hugo Well, it was a sort of experiment, really. They were trying to answer the question: do men and women cook differently?

Kim Really? So what did they do to try to find the answer?

Hugo They invited a male cook and a female cook to prepare five different courses of a meal. Both cooks had to use the same main ingredient for each course, but they didn't have to make the same dish. Then, they served the dishes to a panel of judges, who tasted them, and decided if they were made by the man or the woman.

Kim Who were the judges?

Hugo Well, there were two men and two women. They were all food experts – either chefs themselves or restaurant critics.

Kim What about the cooks? Were they professionals, too?

Hugo Yes. They were from two of the best restaurants in the country.

Kim And what kinds of things did they cook?

Hugo All kinds of things really, but the only ones I remember are a meat dish with garlic and a bright pink dessert.

Kim What was so special about those two dishes?

Hugo I remember them because the judges had real problems deciding if they were made by the male chef or the female chef. In the end, they all got it wrong!

Kim So, did they manage to answer the question, then? Do men cook differently from women?

Hugo Not really. The only conclusion they came to was that it was impossible to tell if a particular dish was made by a man or a woman. That's all, really.

Kim So, it was a waste of time then, really.

Hugo No, it wasn't! I really enjoyed the show, even if they didn't answer the question!

9 A))

Newsreader And our final story on tonight's program is about an Australian diver who has survived a shark attack. 46-year-old Eric Nerhus was fishing off the coast of Cape Howe, New South Wales, when a great white shark attacked him. He was under the water at the time, and he didn't see the animal swimming towards him. Mr. Nerhus's head, shoulders, and one of his arms ended up in the shark's mouth, but, fortunately, he was wearing a heavy metal vest. When the shark tried to bite the man in half, its teeth hit the vest and not his body. Mr. Nerhus knew he had to do something, so he felt for the shark's eye with the hand of his other arm. When he found it, he surprised the animal by pressing his fingers into its eye. The shark reacted by opening its mouth, giving Mr. Nerhus a chance to escape. Despite his injuries, Eric managed to swim up to the surface of the water. His son pulled him onto his boat, and took him quickly to the shore. Meanwhile, another friend called emergency services. Mr. Nerhus was flown to a hospital by helicopter. He had deep cuts all over his body and a broken nose, but he was very lucky to be alive. Attacks by great white sharks usually result in death because of their size and strength. The shark that attacked Mr. Nerhus was over nine feet long.

9 B))

Host Hello, and welcome to the program. Today, we have psychologist, Dr. Chris Hopper, in the studio with us to answer your questions about phobias. Hello, Chris.

Chris Good morning.

Host And our first caller is Cynthia Sharp from San Diego. What's your question, Cynthia?

Cynthia Um, hello, Dr. Hopper. Um, my question is actually about my son, James. He's six years old, and he had a bad experience with a dog last night.

Chris I'm sorry to hear that, Cynthia. What exactly happened?

Cynthia Well, we were outside a neighbor's house, and, um, I was talking with the mom when one of her dogs ran out. It was a big dog, um, and it came running out of the house barking. James panicked, and tried to hide behind me, but the dog jumped on him and bit him. It wasn't a serious injury, but we're very worried that he'll be afraid of dogs now. We don't want him to get a phobia. What should we do?

Chris Well, Cynthia, you're right to be worried about this incident because cynophobia, that is, a fear of dogs, is often caused by a bad experience with a dog as a child. The best thing you can do is to give your son a positive experience with a different dog as soon as possible. If you have any friends who have a quiet and friendly dog, go and visit them. Let your son touch the dog if he wants to and don't remind him about his bad experience.

Host That sounds like good advice, Chris. And our next caller is Natalie Williams from Seattle. Natalie?

9 C))

Host Hello, and welcome to those of you who just joined us. Continuing on our theme of celebrity families, the focus of today's program is actress and singer, Judy Garland, and her daughter, Liza Minnelli.

Now, Judy Garland's real name was Frances Ethel Gumm, and she was born on June 10, 1922 in Grand Rapids, Minnesota. Her parents ran a theater and Judy first appeared on stage singing a Christmas song with her two older sisters when she was two years old. When she was 13, Judy joined the movie company Metro Goldwyn Mayer and at the age of 16, she played Dorothy in *The Wizard of Oz*. The movie was extremely successful, and she won a children's Oscar for her performance. Metro Goldwyn Mayer terminated her

contract in 1950. However, she continued to perform, and in 1964 she did a series of concerts at the London Palladium. In fact, it was in London where Judy Garland was found dead in 1969. Judy got married five times and had three children. One of these children was Liza Minnelli who was 23 when her mother died.

Liza was born in Hollywood, California, on March 12, 1946. She grew up in movie studios, and, like her mother, made her first stage appearance at the age of two. She was only five when her parents got divorced. After performing successfully with her mother at the London Palladium in 1964, Liza became a professional nightclub singer. She made several albums, and later starred as a singer in the 1972 movie, *Cabaret*, a role for which she won an Oscar. Despite her successful singing and acting career, Liza has had similar problems to her mother. She has been married four times, but, unlike her mother, she never had children. Today, Liza Minnelli is in her sixties, but she still makes occasional television appearances.

10 A))

Host Hello, and welcome to the program. Today we have scientist, Doug McLeod, in the studio with us. He's going to tell us about some of the everyday things we know and love that were invented by accident. Doug?

Doug Hello, Janet. Well, I'm going to start with the microwave oven. In 1945, an engineer named Percy Spencer was testing some new radar equipment. He had a chocolate bar in his pocket, and while he was standing in front of the machine, it melted. After that, he also tried using the microwaves from the radar equipment to cook popcorn. Percy realized that microwaves could heat and cook food, and so the microwave oven was born.

Host How interesting! What else do you have for us, Doug?

Doug Next is something that is found in hospitals all over the world: the x-ray machine. In 1895, a German physicist named Wilhelm Roentgen was experimenting with electrical rays in a dark room. He was directing them through a glass tube covered with black paper. Suddenly, he saw a light on a screen on the wall and he realized that the rays could pass through the glass and the paper. After that, he experimented with his own hand, and found that he could see the bones. The first x-ray ever made was an image of Roentgen's wife's hand – you can even see her wedding ring!

Host That's fascinating, Doug. We have time for one more.

Doug Many different kinds of food were discovered by accident, Janet, and I've chosen something that we call potato chips, but the British call crisps. These were invented by a chef named George Crum, who was working in a restaurant near Saratoga Springs, New York. A customer complained that the French fries he was served were too thick. The chef was angry about this, so he fried some very thin potatoes and covered them with salt. The customer loved them, and after that Saratoga Chips became popular all over the US. Eventually, they were produced for people to eat at home.

Host That was all very fascinating, Doug. Thanks for joining us.

10 B))

Tony Amy, did you study foreign languages in high school?

Amy Yes, I did. Actually, I used to be really good at languages.

Tony Which ones did you study?

Amy Well, I took French for five years, and then I took Japanese for six years, and I studied Spanish for a year during my lunch break.

Tony And how much French can you remember?

Amy Not much! But I can remember my Japanese, because I took it for my degree in college. Why all the questions, Tony?

Tony Well, I've just read this article about the state of language learning in schools in the US, and it isn't looking good. It says that adults only remember about seven words from the languages they studied at school.

Amy Only seven words? That isn't very good, is it? What kinds of words do they remember?

Tony Common words, like *hello, goodbye, please, thank you, one, two,* and *three,* and the question *Do you speak English?*

Amy So, what happens when people are abroad? Do they practice the language?

Tony Not at all. In fact, the article suggests that people often choose not to go on vacation to countries where they have to worry about language problems.

Amy That's probably because they're too lazy to learn a language.

Tony No, it isn't that. The article says it's because they're too embarrassed to try and speak it.

Amy OK. So which languages do students study in school today?

Tony Hang on a minute, there's a list here somewhere… Here it is. It says 50% of students study Spanish, 25% study French, 22% study Japanese, and 2% Russian. Arabic is becoming more popular, too.

Amy And what are schools going to do about the problem?

Tony Well, first of all, they're going to introduce language classes for children in elementary schools. And then they're going to start offering languages from around the world, for example Mandarin Chinese and Urdu.

Amy That sounds difficult. Anyway, Tony, which languages did you use to study at school?

Tony Only French. And I was terrible at it!

10 C))

Speaker 1 I made a bad decision once when I was traveling home to Washington, D.C. from college in Boston, a trip of almost 450 miles. The choice was going by train or by bus, and I opted for the train because it was quicker. Unfortunately, the train broke down on the way, so in the end I took two hours longer than I expected.

Speaker 2 The worst decision I ever made was giving my son a skateboard for his tenth birthday. On the morning of his birthday, we went down to the park to try it out. Sadly, he fell off the board as soon as he got on it, and broke his arm. We had to cancel his birthday party, and we spent the whole day in the hospital instead.

Speaker 3 I had two interviews and both companies offered me a job. In the first job, they offered me more money, but it was a long way from where I live – an hour traveling every day. The second job was less money, but it was very close to my house. In the end, I chose the second job instead, and I'm very happy I did, because last month the first company closed down.

Speaker 4 One time, I had to decide between a good friend of mine and a boy I really liked. I was going to a concert with my friend, and then this boy asked me to go to the movies with him on the same night. In the end, I said no to the boy, and went to the concert with my friend. I found out later that the boy already had a girlfriend, so I think I made the right decision.

Speaker 5 You won't believe what happened to me! I buy coffee from the same coffee shop every day. One day, I was late for work, so I didn't stop at the coffee shop. Of course, that was the day the coffee shop was celebrating its ten-year anniversary. It gave away tickets for ten-free drinks! Everyone in my office got the tickets, but me!

11 A))

Speaker 1 The worst loser I know is my mom. We often used to play cards together when I was little, and if my mom was losing, it was safer to stop playing. She was always happy when she was winning, but when she was losing, you could see her getting angrier and angrier until she exploded. Sometimes, she used to go out of the room because she was so upset!

Speaker 2 I once had a friend who was a bad loser at tennis. In fact, we stopped talking to each other because of a tennis match. We were about twenty at the time, and on this occasion we were arguing over a point. I said the ball was out and she said it was in. In the end, she just threw her racket into the net and left. We haven't spoken since.

Speaker 3 I have to be very careful at work when we're talking about ice hockey. I have a colleague who gets really upset when his team loses, and he hates it if you make a joke about it. I tried it once, and he just stood up, walked out, and closed the door with a bang. He didn't speak to me for days after that, so I don't think I'll try it again.

Speaker 4 My son is a very bad loser, in fact he always has been. He's 12 now, but he still hates losing. We used to play board games together when he was little, but he always used to cry if he didn't win. I had to choose between letting him win all the time, or making him upset if I won. In the end, I stopped playing that kind of game with him.

Speaker 5 One of the guys who plays basketball with me gets incredibly upset during games, and he spends most of the time shouting at the other players. He's a really nervous person at the best of times, but when we're losing, it really is too much. The referee throws him off the court at least twice a month, and once our coach told him to go home.

11 B))

Interviewer Can I ask you about your job, Jerry?

Jerry Yes, of course. Go ahead.

Interviewer What time do you go to bed?

Jerry Well, I don't often get home before six o'clock in the morning, and it usually takes me a little while to relax. It's probably about seven by the time I go to sleep.

Interviewer And what time do you have to get up again?

Jerry I usually get up at one o'clock, to have lunch with my family. After that, I go back to bed again for an hour or so, until about three o'clock.

Interviewer Do you need an alarm clock to wake up?

Jerry No, I never use one. I wake up the first time when my children come home from school for lunch. The second time, my wife wakes me up. That's when I get up for good.

Interviewer How do you feel when you wake up?

Jerry It depends on the day, really. If I've only worked for a day or two, I'm full of energy, but if it's after the fifth or sixth night in a row, I'm absolutely exhausted. That's when I find it really hard to get out of bed.

Interviewer What do you do about meals, Jerry?

Jerry Well, like I said, my first meal of the day is what you would call lunch. Then, I have dinner at about midnight with some other drivers in a cafe. When I get home in the morning, I have something light, like a cheese sandwich or some toast before I go to bed.

Interviewer Would you like to change your working hours, Jerry?

Jerry If I changed my working hours, I wouldn't earn as much money! There's a lot more work at night because people go out for dinner and to the theater or movies, and then it's late and they need to get home, and they don't want to drive because they're tired. I enjoy my job, really, because I meet a lot of interesting people.

11 C))

Host And to finish off today's program, we're going to take a look at some famous twins. Let's start with probably the earliest set of twins in history: Romulus and Remus. Now, the legend says that they were abandoned by their parents because twins were thought to bring bad luck. Fortunately, they were found by a female wolf, which looked after them when they were babies. According to legend, the boys grew up, and later founded the city of Rome. After some time, they began to argue, and eventually Romulus killed Remus. As Romulus was the only brother alive, the city was called Rome after him.

Let's move on in history to the 1950s, when a set of twins named the Kray Brothers caused a lot of trouble in London's East End. Ronnie and Reggie Kray were both nightclub owners. They had expensive lifestyles, and through their nightclubs they met several American stars like Frank Sinatra and Judy Garland.

However, they were also extremely violent people, and they committed many illegal crimes in the city. They were involved in many robberies and murders until they were eventually arrested in 1969. They were both sent to prison for life, and they both died when they were in their sixties.

On a happier note, the youngest twins ever to become famous are the Olsen twins. Mary Kate and Ashley Olsen were given the same role on the American TV series *Full House* when they were only six months old. They played the part of a little girl, and they played the same part for eight years. The producers used both sisters to play the same part so that they didn't break the law on the number of hours a child could work. The show was very popular with American audiences. Today, the twins have grown up, and they have a fashion business.

And I'm afraid that's all we have time for. Join me, Roy Thompson, at 4 o'clock tomorrow afternoon for another two hours of *Thompson's Choice*. Bye for now.

12 A))

Newsreader And now it's time for the news. A Florida couple's cell phones were stolen while they were visiting family last week. Mary and Richard Ranieri had left their car unlocked, and someone took their cell phones. Luckily, one of the cell phones had a GPS tracking device. The couple tracked the cell phone to a nearby home. The Ranieris called the police and an officer went to the house. He talked to a man whose grandson had arrived home just after the cell phones had been stolen. The grandson told the officer he hadn't taken the phones, but a few minutes later, someone called the phones, and they began ringing from a closet in the grandson's room.

A tourist had a lucky escape yesterday while she was bungee jumping off the Victoria Falls in Zambia. Twenty-two-year-old Erin Langworthy fell into the river because her bungee rope had broken when she jumped. She landed in the water with her feet still tied to the broken rope, and then she swam to safety. Ms. Langworthy was taken straight to the hospital after the accident, but had no serious injuries.

A Swedish woman has found the white gold wedding ring that she lost over 16 years ago. Lena Paahlsson had taken off the ring while she was cooking with her daughters. When she went to put it back on again, it had disappeared. That is, until yesterday, when she was picking vegetables in her garden, and she found the ring around a carrot. The ring doesn't fit Mrs. Paahlsson any more, but she is going to have it made bigger.

An Australian woman had a frightening experience last night, when she discovered an adult crocodile in her living room. Forty-two-year-old Jo Dodd got out of bed when she heard her dog barking. When she opened the bedroom door, she saw a crocodile in the middle of the room. Mrs. Dodd woke her husband, who called the local Crocodile Management Center, and a crocodile catcher came to take the animal away. The crocodile had escaped from a nearby crocodile farm earlier in the week.

And that's all for now. I'll be back again at 9 o'clock for the next news update.

12 B))

Alan Who do you think gossips more, Jessica? Men or women?

Jessica Well, I gossip a lot with my female colleagues at work, so I suppose that women are the biggest gossips. What do you think?

Alan Yes, that's what I thought, too, but it says here that it's actually men who are the biggest gossips. That's what the results of this survey say, anyway.

Jessica What survey?

Alan This one here in the newspaper. It says the survey was carried out by a telecommunications company. They wanted to do research into gossiping for a new service they're offering. The aim of the survey was to find out what kind of people enjoy gossiping, and how much time they spend doing it.

Jessica So what did they find out?

Alan Well, they had a big surprise. The study showed that a fifth of the men they interviewed said they spent at least three hours a day gossiping.

Jessica Wow! That's a lot! And where do they usually gossip?

Alan Most of them said they usually gossiped at work. Hang on…I can give you the exact figures. Yes, …55 percent of the men said they gossiped at work compared to 46 percent of the women.

Jessica Goodness! I didn't realize men had so much to say! Did they tell the researchers what they usually talked about?

Alan Yes. They said that their main topics of conversation were their women colleagues, and who in the company would get the next promotion.

Jessica The part about women colleagues doesn't surprise me in the least. So, what about the women in the survey? Did they say what they talked about?

Alan Yes, they did. They told the researchers that they talked about the problems they were having in their families. They also chatted about what was happening in their favorite TV series.

Jessica OK. So what about you, Alan? Do you ever gossip at work?

Alan What? Me? No, never! I wouldn't dream of it!

12 C))

Speaker 1 I used to watch a quiz show called *What's My Line?* It was a funny show. Four celebrity panelists asked a contestant questions about his or her occupation. The contestant could only answer "yes" or "no." After asking several questions, the panelists had to guess the contestant's job. Sometimes there was a mystery guest such as a famous actor or musician. Instead of naming the mystery guest's occupation, the panelists had to guess the mystery guest's name.

Speaker 2 My favorite quiz show is *Cash Cab*. It takes place in a moving New York City cab. The contestants are people who actually want to take a cab someplace. When they get in the cab, the driver—who's the host—asks them questions during the ride. If the contestants answer the questions correctly, they win money. If they get three answers wrong, they have to leave the cab. My favorite kind of question is a "red-light challenge" where contestants have to think of as many answers as possible to a question.

Speaker 3 I used to listen to *Wait Wait…Don't Tell Me!*; a radio news program with a few news quizzes added for fun. There were always three celebrity panelists who made jokes about the news. One quiz I particularly enjoyed was *Bluff the Listener*. A contestant listens to three silly, but related, news items that are read by the panelists. Two of the stories aren't true, and one story is an actual news story. The listener has to guess which story is true.

Speaker 4 I've always enjoyed the quiz show *Who wants to be a Millionaire?* It started in the US in 1999, and it's still on TV today. In each show, one contestant is asked a series of questions, and they have to choose the right answer out of four possible options. It's pretty exciting, really, because the contestant can win up to a million dollars if they're good.

Speaker 5 My favorite quiz show when I was a teenager was *Rock & Roll Jeopardy!* It wasn't on for long – only a couple of years – but I used to love it. There were three contestants who had to answer questions about rock music, but the answers had to be in the form of a question. Each question was worth a different amount of money, and the winning player got his or her score in cash. I used to watch it every week.

General Manager: Laura Pearson
Executive Publishing Manager: Erik Gundersen
Senior Managing Editor: Louisa van Houten
Associate Editor: Hana Yoo
Design Director: Susan Sanguily
Executive Design Manager: Maj-Britt Hagsted
Associate Design Manager: Michael Steinhofer
Image Manager: Trisha Masterson
Image Editor: Liaht Pashayan
Electronic Production Manager: Julie Armstrong
Production Coordinator: Brad Tucker

ACKNOWLEDGEMENTS

The authors and publisher are grateful to those who have given permission to reproduce the following extracts and adaptations of copyright material:

p.9 Extract from 'Fleurs Fraîches' by Heidi Ellison, 19 October 2010. © Heidi Ellison, ParisUpdate.com. Reproduced by permission; p.16 Extract from 'My loaf saver: Woman's life is saved by bag of sliced white bread as it stops her head smashing against crashed car' by Luke Salkeld, *The Daily Mail*, 26 November 2011. Reproduced by permission of Solo Syndication; p.16 Extract from 'Man's life saved by heroic DVD', www.metro.co.uk. Reproduced by permission of Solo Syndication; p.25 Extract from 'Research: women will be doing the housework until 2050' by Tim Ross, *The Telegraph*, 20 May 2011. © Telegraph Media Group Limited 2011; p.40 Extract from 'Tourist Scam Alert'. © 2012 www.ricksteves.com, used with permission; p.44 Extract from 'Mothers-in-law are lovely in their place. Their own place, that is' by Luisa Dillner, *The Independent*, 28 February 2010. Reproduced by permission; p.48 Extract from 'Apple Teams Up To Use iPhone to Save Cherokee Language' by Murray Evans. Reproduced by permission of Associated Press; p.66 Extract from 'David Suchet remembers his school sporting achievements and the teacher who inspired him to pursue acting' by Tim Oglethorpe, *The Daily Mail Weekend Magazine*, 24 October 2009. Reproduced by permission of Solo Syndication; p.66 Extract from 'Bonjour is about all we learn from 5 years of French' by Laura Clark, *The Daily Mail*, 02 August 2007. Reproduced by permission of Solo Syndication; p.68 Extract from 'No need to sleep on this one: A good night's rest really does help you make important decisions', *The Daily Mail*, 20 June 2011. Reproduced by permission of Solo Syndication.

Illustrations by: Cover: Chellie Carroll; Peter Bull pp. 47, bottom 49; Atsushi Hara/Dutch Uncle Agency pp. 13, 24, 25, 39, 50, 54; Satoshi Hashimoto/Dutch Uncle Agency p.69; Tim Marrs pp.22, 24, 42; Jérôme Mireault/Colagene Illustrations pp. 28, 31, 40, 70; Ellis Nadler pp.28, 34, 51, 81; Roger Penwill pp.37, 47 top, 71; Kath Walker Illustration pp.16, 17, 45, 52, 69 top, 76, 77.

We would also like to thank the following for permission to reproduce the following photographs: Cover: Gemenacom/shutterstock.com; Andrey_Popov/shutterstock.com; Wavebreakmedia/shutterstock.com; Image Source/Getty Images; Lane Oatey/Blue Jean Images/Getty Images; BJI/Blue Jean Images/Getty Images; Image Source/Corbis; Yuri Arcurs/Tetra Images/Corbis; Wavebreak Media Ltd./Corbis; pg. 5 Yellow Dog Productions/Getty Images; pg. 6 MBI/Alamy; pg. 7 Aly Song/REUTERS; pg. 8 (1 Down) Hugh Threlfall/Alamy, (2 Down) Ruslan Kudrin/Alamy, (3 Down) MMStudios, (6 Down) Peter Jobst/Alamy, (4, 7 Down, 3, 5, 10 Across) Gareth Boden, (8 Across) MMStudios, (9 Across) mediablitzimages (uk) Limited/Alamy; (painting) Sunday Afternoon on the Island of La Grande Jatte, 1884–86 (oil on canvas), Seurat, Georges Pierre (1859–91)/ The Art Institute of Chicago, IL, USA/The Bridgeman Art Library (also used pg. 9); pg. 10 Lester Lefkowitz/Getty Images; pg. 11 (1) Westend 61/REX Features, (2) Robert Stainforth/Alamy, (3) RCWW, Inc./Corbis, (4) OUP/Stockbyte, (5) Sipa Press/Rex Features, (6) A. Inden/Corbis, (7) Dan Callister/Rex Features, (8) Michael Blann/Getty Images, (9) Blickwinkel/AGE fotostock, (10) Juice Images/Alamy; pg. 12 (1) Kniel Synnatzschke/ Getty Images, (2) Brad Wilson/Getty Images, (3) Kindler, Andreas/Getty Images, (4) Gabe Palmer/Getty Images, (5) Alan Graf/Getty Images; pg. 15 Jacob Halaska/Getty Images; pg. 16 SWNS South west News Service; pg. 18 Bloomberg via Getty Images; pg. 19 Ocean/ Corbis; pg. 20 (Prague) Joe Cornish/Getty Images, (Vienna) Tibor Bognar/Corbis, (Budapest) Keith MacGregor/Getty Images; pg. 23 (paella) Dorling Kindersly/Getty Images, (theaters) Ben Pipe/The Travel Library/Rex Features, (fish) Atlantide Phototravel/ Corbis; pg. 26 FI Online/Rex Features; pg. 29 (juggle) Art Vandalay/Getty Images, (bread) Plattform/Johnér Images/Corbis, (monoploy) Franz-Peter Tschauner/dpa/ Corbis, (shelf) PM Images/Getty Images; pg. 32 David Buffington/Spaces Images/Corbis; pg. 33 (Salvador) dbimages/Alamy, (Sugar Loaf) Jane Sweeney/JAI/Corbis, (museum) age fotostock/SuperStock, (beach) Mark Leibowitz/Masterfile; pg. 35 Davies and Starr/ Getty Images; pg. 36 Alex Segre/Rex Features; pg. 38 Leon/Getty Images; pg. 41 Jose Luis Pelaez Inc./Getty Images; pg. 44 MBI/Alamy; pg. 46 Geoff Moore/Getty Images; pg. 48 (class) Ken Seet/Corbis, (ipod) Dirk Lindner/Corbis, (laptop) Scott Hortop/Alamy, (kindle) Alex Segre/Rex Features; pg. 51 Tom Grill/Tetra Images/Corbis; pg. 53 (earthquake, fire, hurricane) AFP/Getty Images, (blizzard) Esch Collection/Getty Images; pg. 55 (Adria) Britta Pedersen/dpa/Corbis, (Escoffier) Hulton-Deutsch Collection/Corbis, (Oliver) Erik Pendzich/Rex Features, (Colicchio) Gilbert Carrasquillo/FilmMagic/Getty Images, (Morimoto) Stephen Lovekin/WireImage for Gourmet Magazine/Getty Images; pg. 56 (2 across) Peter Cade/Getty Images, (6, 7 across) Paul Souders/Getty Images, (9 across) Paul Oomen/Getty Images, (10 Across) Visuals Unlimited,Inc./John Abbott/Getty Images, (1 Down) Suchitra prints/Hgetty Images, (3 Down) OUP/Eureka, (4 Down) Wolfgang Kumm/dpa/Corbis, (5 down) Danita Delimont/Getty Images, (8 down) Kelly Funk/ Getty Images; pg. 58 Jon Kopaloff/FilmMagic/Getty Images; pg. 59 Nick Ridley/Getty Images; pg. 60 Asia Images Group Pte Ltd/Alamy; pg. 61 (John Lennon) Brian Hamill/ Getty Images, (Julian Lennon) Kevin Knight/Corbis, (Sean Lennon) Astrid Stawiarz/ Getty Images, (Garland) Eric Carpenter/John Kobal Foundation/Getty Images, (Minnelli) Mike Stephens/Central Press/Getty Images; pg. 62 Walter Bibikow/Getty Images; pg. 63 (plane) Allison Joyce/Getty Images, (Saturn) OUP/Photodisc, (Iron Lady) Film 4/The Kobal Collection, (phone) OUP/Dunca Daniel Mihai, (gas) OUP/Photographers Choice, (Petronas) ULTRA.F/Getty Images, (Avatar) Twentieth Century-Fox Film Corporation/ The Kobal Collection, (mini cooper) Martyn Goddard/Corbis; pg. 64 (microwave) OUP/D. Hurst, (chips) Brian Hagiwara/Getty Images, (xray) Scott Camazine/Alamy; pg. 66 ITV/Rex Features; pg. 72 Diane Diederich/Getty Images; pg. 73 Scott Markewitz/ Getty Images; pg. 74 (India) Niklas Hallen/Barcroft Media, (Italy) LatitudeStock - Justin Williams/Getty Images, (Olsens) Billy Farrell Agency/Rex Features, (Krays) William Lovelace/Getty Images; pg. 75 (UK flag) OUP/EyeWire, (US flag) OUP/Image Farm; pg. 78 (young girls) Ulrik Tofte/Getty Images, (senior women) Corbis Premium RF/Alamy, (men) Yellow Dog Productions/Getty Images.